PEREGRINE WATCHING

Peregrine Watching

by

Ron Berry

Gomer Press
1987

First Impression - July 1987

ISBN 0 86383 362 4

Printed in Wales by Gomer Press, Llandysul, Dyfed

In Memory of
RAY LISLE: 1927–1976

Other Books by Ron Berry

HUNTERS AND HUNTED
TRAVELLING LOADED
THE FULL-TIME AMATEUR
FLAME AND SLAG
SO-LONG, HECTOR BEBB

Facing north, the escarpment overlooks a cold, deep reservoir. Scree gutters rise from the shoreline to the crags. These are blue pennant sandstone, tussocked, mossed, ivied, layered with whinberry bushes, heather, and sprigged all over with starved rowans and silver birches. Above the escarpment, 15-20-year-old sitka spruces cover the mountains as far as the eye can see. Down below, beyond the dam wall, more sitkas on what was once a large, rolling common. Here in Wales, the Forestry Commission has effected a land-grab greater than any since the Roman invasions. Horizons have been degraded, watersheds obliterated, deciduous copses overwhelmed. When the conifers are harvested in the next century, areas of ancient Gwalia will look like the Western Front, reeking of diesel instead of cordite.

Watching peregrines becomes obsessional. We logged almost 300 hours between the three of us. Allan and Doug are brothers; apart from the peregrine connection they seem to have little in common. I first saw the tiercel on 18th April, '79. He went bulleting down, up and crosswise, chivvying a pair of ravens who were feeding hefty youngsters in a nest around the massive frontal boss of a buttress, less than ten yards from the eyrie as it turned out. But we had to find a vantage point. At the edge of a block of conifers adjacent to the reservoir, an old sheepfold, two pounds with walls higher than a man, and the ruins of a dwelling place where, maybe, shepherds of two centuries ago praised God via Williams Pantycelyn hymns. They prompted wonder, those monoglot shepherds, times having shifted from rustic jogtrot to space satellites.

The larger pound gave us a view of the whole escarpment. The eyrie was 300 yards away. We were obeying the first principle of peregrine-watching. On 19th April we did a combined watch of six hours. At 9.20 a.m. *two* tiercels and a falcon flew high above the water. Cross tracking and swinging tangents, they vanished like bees in a tumbling moraine of northern cloud. We couldn't determine which tiercel was mated to the falcon.

I was back in the sheepfold by noon the following day. The tiercel came tight-winged from the left, arrowing below the skyline to a flat rock near a bark-skinned rowan. He stood there for 35 minutes. Then he flew out fast above the conifers, only to return a few minutes later to his perch. He took off at 3.15 p.m., winging along the waterside and over the dam wall. He came back to a moley tump above the central buttress. Now he ruffled his feathers, he preened assiduously, breast, rump, thighs, hooking up his carpels to comb through the fish-belly grey barring. He looked all fluffed out and humped; he'd taken a bath in the outflow brook from the reservoir. Winnowing some white feathers from his breast, he stroked them off his beak. His throat shone like a soap advert. The yellow of his feet gleamed as if glycerined. He stopped preening at 4.30 p.m., although occasionally he roused or probed under a wing—the task of perfection. I left at 5 o'clock, bone-perished and sore-bottomed.

21st April, 6 p.m., and a bladder of sun rolling at a creep along the horizon, making it impossible to use binoculars unless a cloud masked the glare. By naked eye I saw the tiercel flying low inside the escarpment and out over the far side. Two men were fishing below the great central buttress. At 7.5 p.m. the falcon came in from the west, sheared over the mountain top, swerved at a panicked wheatear and pitched on a projecting spur some yards beyond the tiercel's look-out stand. As she floated across to the grassy deck outside the scrape, I saw the tiercel shooting up from a gully like a small anti-gravity bomb. The falcon lowered herself and waddled out of sight. Delight tingled. She was down on eggs.

The tiercel travelled west, and the ravens carried full pouches to their young. It was a wintry April. Frogs were still coupled in ditches as I plodded back to the car.

Rain all day on 23rd April. The following morning I found the tiercel on a new perch, his back to the wide vale. Unless he turned his head he was invisible. Matching their eyeball-shimmering speed, peregrines have a dauntless capacity for stillness. I nudged the telescope with my knuckles while lighting a cigarette, lost the tiercel, then heard him screaming three times. It was 1 o'clock. He went to the eyrie a few minutes later, looked in at the hidden falcon, swung out from the rock face and rose to his perch by the rowan.

Wheatears squirted over the scree, their courtship songs like dry rubber squeegees. At 2.55 p.m. the tiercel sparred with the ravens, scything dives and caracoles accompanying tearing screams. We came to anticipate these skirmishes as preliminaries to nest-relief. The incubating peregrine, we decided, might be somewhat dopey, in need of protection—however, this is a Lilliputian's theory. The tiercel perched nearer the sheepfold, but not for long. His urgent hekking brought out the falcon and they chased off another, or the same stray tiercel as on 18th April. Two minutes later the falcon shot straight back to her eggs.

This immemorial land of my fathers seemed to be rife with peregrines. I spent a day visiting two pre-War peregrine sites, towering cirques, the first overlooking conifers, the other above landscaped pit-slag. Engineered aesthetics for industrialised Wales are often arse-backwards. Tips (greened-over tips sometimes) are bulldozed, contoured, guaranteeing to leave the hand of man smudged large for evermore as far as time counts, prettied with red-ash footpaths, alien grasses, pseudo-rustic footbridges spanning tiny streams, forestry haulage roads and more spruces and larches.

The cirques were empty, ravens in situ, mattock beaks profiled against the sky. I saw three pairs of kestrels, a lone buzzard, ring-ouzels (we call them quarry blackbirds), crows, magpies, wheatears and wrens.

I enjoyed the next watch with Allan. He's uncannily intense, detecting nuances of calls and songs like a conductor of symphonies. Allan plays the trumpet. Sun above the escarpment as we expected. Cold and blustery. We damned the blinding horizon. Bird-men are not all fearlessly urbane, punditic like the numbing talking heads of television. We saw the tiercel clipping over the mountain top. At 7.40 p.m. he hung in the wind above us on our side of the escarpment, slowly drifting, waiting on for eight minutes, cut into the sky, unlike the flickering feathered air-dancing of a kestrel. Only his head moved. He watched us too, oddly headless, just a stubby ripple fronting the bow-rake of his wings. Suddenly he geared into force, a piling stoop towards the eyrie. The woodpigeon twisted close to the rocks, down a gully and crashed into the conifers. Waiting on again, the tiercel veered higher, higher, then abruptly tipped into stooping at 60 degrees,

twisting into an inevitable crawling torque. We didn't witness the end of it. Allan sang, "Jesus!" and I muttered, "Christ."

For three seasons we had watched peregrines in Powys. We had memories of stoops flung down the sky at long, long range. We had seen many kills brought in, and the maiden flight of an eyas.

Allan said, "That was the best yet."

26th April, 10.30 a.m., the tiercel upright on the rock shelf by the rowan. He left for an hour. Next I saw him walking on brown shale to his mole-tump. At 12.25 p.m. he launched out to meet a small flock of pigeons. I think he first saw them puffing free from a village loft two miles beyond the lowland conifers. Suspiciously negligent, he split the flock from below and levelled off above the sheep-fold. The pigeons bundled hectically over the scree. He clipped past the eyrie, only inches from the rock face, then he winged fast over the top of the mountain. Twenty minutes later he dropped back on his tump. From here he dived directly on what appeared to be the same small flock of homers, again without making contact. He perched briefly and flew west, knifing along the skyline as if mechanised.

Doug vexed, ageing himself. He considered our tiercel a pretty duff raptor. Soon there'd be chicks needing regular supplies of raw meat.

Two days later twelve hang-gliders, airborne in batches of four, were active in the area. Hang-gliders are heroes, theirs is Cloud 9, they have followers, helpers who read the wind, clock times, take photographs; when they aren't disciples, presumably they function socially. We worried about the peregrines. I sent bluntish reports to the R.S.P.B.

Dense fog ruined most of 29th April. Allan abandoned an early morning session. Endless fog like crawling ectoplasm bulged across the cliffs, wispier stuff extending down the steep slope of whinberry and scree to the water's edge. During a gusty break in the murk I saw the falcon on her tufted projecting rock near the eyrie. She leaned into the wind, wings and tail flared wide. The tiercel was incubating but I failed to see the change-over. On 30th April the tiercel landed on a new perch as I creaked into the sheepfold. He made three vertical dives in front of the eyrie at 7.45 p.m. and rose back to his tump look-out. Two anglers were yelling at each other across a small bay, effing and blinding to jam the ghost of Izaak Walton. The tiercel flew west. At 8.25 p.m. he was back on his flat shelf of rock. Snow and sleet stormed over the water. I felt wry-necked. My limbs were Frankensteinian.

More than an inch of snow fell on the night of 1st May. Twenty miles away, Powys hills remained white all day, glazed like majolica, a vista for polar bears and wolverines. A half-grown hare, ears cocked, lolloped through the sopping-wet feathers of last year's bog-fed grasses. New-born lambs had the crimped trembles of grotesques on the brink of survival.

I heard the delirious tikk-tikking of kestrels. They were copulating on a ledge behind a slanting silver birch, less than one hundred yards above the sheep-fold. The female went shrilling after a ring ouzel. She came back to perch in the tree. We gazed at each other. Her face had the bruised downcast look of a victim, sad spouse of a wife-beater. This is anthropomorphic fancy of course. The kestrels went ringing up above the mountain until they were dots, male and female swinging towards and away from each other. Conspicuously silent, the ravens hustled, arriving from below or above, feeding their youngsters snugged in enough smelly wool to knit a baby's cardigan.

I saw a nest-relief. The falcon came driving in across the reservoir, swept up the buttress, the ravens flinging away from her like burial rags. She landed on a crag for seconds and looped down and upwards to the eyrie. A peregrine's mode of copping. The tiercel shot out, skied himself in a great Ferris wheel, and from somewhere near the apex of his ascent a silenced skylark dropped safely to earth. The tiercel perched on shale. After a while he began preening.

I called in Doug's house on the way home. He performed on the pastelblue wall-to-wall carpet of his living room, miming a peregrine, flexing, scratching, stretching, his arm and leg held out, quivering, his head turning, glaring, searching—Doug has a hawkish nose.

3rd May. Sunshine and showers. At 2.30 p.m. the falcon came in from the west and flew south. She returned after an hour, perched twice and tightened into hunting flight way out over the conifers. Distance claimed her. Before relieving the tiercel 30 minutes later, she harassed the ravens. The tiercel stood on his tump. This seemed to be a genuine pattern, perhaps due to the proximity of the nesting ravens. The bird from the eyrie would re-orient itself before leaving the escarpment. Physiological perhaps (again), related to incubation. When he took wing the tiercel climbed, ringing up, all sky in his blood and bones, as he drifted away to the west. He came back to a rock face opposite the central buttress at 4.14 p.m. He was still there when I left at 7 o'clock. We had to believe kills were made away from the escarpment, at half light of dawn and dusk.

Allan climbed into the pound at 6.40 p.m. on 4th May. I had located the tiercel squatting motionless on a stony sheep-track above the eyrie. He flew east and reappeared 25 minutes later from the north, angling sharply westward, below the horizon as usual. He landed outside the nest-scrape for seconds (Allan detected a soft tchook-tchooking while the two birds were at the eyrie), and flew up to his mole-tump, his white throat dingy in the ashen light. Again it was bitterly cold. My wife mentioned pneumonia, chronic ailments, pain-killing tablets.

Doug kept watch for five hours the following morning. My session began at 5.20 p.m. The tiercel faced the vale from his stand beside the peeled rowan. Fine snow confettied through sunshine. It was ludicrous. The northern sky hung low, massed mill-puff. More snow. Then, from 5.40 to 6.15 p.m., a complete white-out over the escarpment. I sat huddled inside a newish ex-W.D. coat and leggings, head bent to the elements, pretending stoicism. When I was able to raise my binoculars, the tiercel hadn't moved . . . Sun shone like the acquired coquetry of a houri. The hawk slanted down to perch on the rock face. He stayed there for twenty minutes. As I clambered out of the sheepfold over an hour later, I saw him coming in, flapping fast, stumbling, grounding above a heather clump. He had a kill. The feeding hawk merged into sable twigs, snow sprinklings and wet blue pennant.

Until the blizzard changed the landscape, five hang-gliders were floating above the lowland conifers. Meandering aimlessly, they had the emblematic ugliness of pterodactyls.

6th May was less wintry. During his morning watch Doug saw the falcon bringing in a pigeon. She plumed her prey and fed on sparsely mossed shale above the nest. When I arrived in the pound at 5.35 p.m., the tiercel came across the shoreline with a thrush-size carcass. His brief screeching failed to draw the falcon off her eggs. He waited, then simply ripped into the carcass. These hawks have a fiery metabolism. Even

while tearing off ribbons of flesh they appear enhanced by divine edict. They wear that nimbus of sovereignty and project the wonderful paradox of quenchless ferocity and primordial patience.

At 6.15 p.m. the tiercel flew from his ledge by the rowan across to the eyrie. He looked in at the falcon for half a minute before flipping down and around to a lower perch on the near side of the buttress. He hadn't budged when I came away at 8 p.m. During this watch, anxiety calls from a pair of redstarts seeped through my dreaming, *'wheet tik-tik'* from the conifers around the sheepfold. Meanwhile too, the female kestrel began incubating in a scrape hidden behind the slanted silver birch. Always they hunted the far left- hand side of the escarpment and the open hillside out to where the hang-gliders trotted into flight. Soon the redstarts were nesting in a wall of the sheepfold. There were five eggs (five out of six: taken short, she laid one blue egg ten inches away from the nest), so we shifted our location along the block of conifers. Peregrine- watchers have to be inconspicuous and deliberately slow-motion.

10.40 a.m., 8th May. Our falcon tracing horizontal eternity symbols above the reservoir. Yet another damp, lifeless day marking the coldest (1979) cheating Spring this century. She broke free, heading for some unknown target, and returned at 11.25 a.m. to relieve the tiercel. He slewed up to a ledge for the customary adjusting spell, jerked out a greeny-white mute and flew over the mountain. We came away. At least Paul and his wife had seen a nest-relief. I felt glad about that. This Paul, he's a statistician ornithologist, meticulous census-maker in his home patch with records of breeding species, winter migrants, song-cycles, call-notes, times, dates, locations, norms and phenomena extending over eleven years.

Leaving the escarpment we drove, fiddling through Forestry Commission gates, to a small lake set below rocks around the far side of the mountain. Ravens had abandoned a nest; now they were feeding young in a higher, safer nest. On the afternoon of 3rd April, a fall of snow covered the rim of the first nest. The sitting raven was albinoed. Occasionally she stood up to shake snow off herself. Paul trekked around the lake while his wife botanised along the shoreline. He found some pellets below the nest, and the regurgitated shank and foot of a passerine. The parent ravens skulked, flighting short hops from crag to crag. Commonly, when there are eggs, ravens maintain a safe distance from human intruders. They react by gouging out pieces of turf with their great black bills.

Doug and Allan kept watch for the next few days. Doug warned off two men with shotguns and dogs. They were hunting foxes, but the sight of a hawk primes trigger fingers. During my absence the whinberry-covered slope flooded into soft green leaf. The whole escarpment shone, greened in higgledy-piggledy layers. Our route outside the forestry fence was littered with glistening tip-end shucks off the conifers. Two willow warblers were singing, two ring ouzels piping, woodpigeons cooing. The female kestrel sat tight on her eggs. Magpies squawked, and the young ravens just around the buttress from the eyrie, clamoured every time the parent birds brought in food. I found the tiercel perched with his back to the vale, his tail raked inwards like a woodpecker's prop. Twilight brought 60-70 herring gulls sailing around above the water. They cohered and rose clear of the escarpment, a long trundling arc, rising and descending to their roosting place on the small lake beyond the far mountain.

That same evening in Doug's house, he told me about a stray tiercel seen on 13th May. Allan and I saw him, or another loner searching for territory and a mate, on the afternoon of 20th May. It was warmer. We were grateful. At 5.55 p.m. a tiercel flew to a perch opposite the eyrie. He glowed black headed, white throated, delicate grey barring slotted across his belly and breast. Obviously a mature bird. At 6.10 p.m. the falcon came belting out from the nest and harried the perched tiercel, proving he was a strapper, because her bonded mate screamed from somewhere and together they drove him off. The falcon swooped back to her eggs, while our bona fide tiercel copped on his look-out tump. He flew at 6.35 p.m., shooting fast down over the conifers. Three minutes later he returned with a magpie. Just three minutes to kill and carry. He rasped triumphant screams. Some mild diminuendo screams came from the nesting falcon. I had the tiercel focussed in my 'scope. The magpie was plumed in nine minutes. He carried the carcass to his perch by the bark-skinned rowan. It was cached there, tucked in a crevice behind the flat, jutting boulder. Rolling like an African grey parrot, he slugged awkwardly to the edge of the rock and stared across at the eyrie. Eventually he flew to a narrow perch about 7 feet below the nest-scrape. He stayed, married to blue pennant, his tail hanging. Allan hummed to himself in the gloaming as we came away.

But where are the youngsters? By now our peregrines should be feeding chicks, leggy balls of white down gaping and whining for raw meat.

There were twelve cars parked outside the dam wall. Maybe another dozen were hidden by conifers on the approach road. Anglers lounged beside their propped rods, smoking and chatting. Some demoniacs were casting on water gleaming like black alloy, their heavy lines cracking the surface like pit ropes. Windless afternoon of 21st May, no sight or sound of the peregrines. At 6 p.m. two schoolboys rolled stones down the steep shale above the buttress, flushing the tiercel off the nest. He flew south after ringing up a few times. Unaware, the lads wandered back to a forestry road. Twice the tiercel returned in silence, perching only for seconds, then the falcon screamed once and I missed seeing her entering the escarpment. She looked around from the grassy mound outside the scrape, ducked her shoulders and went in. When the tiercel came whipping along below the kestrels' ledge, again in silence, I thought, like Doug: Another try, another failure. This time however he had something small in his foot, already plumed, a tidbit which he gulped down in two minutes.

Lacking experience of watching peregrines during the late Fifties and throughout the Sixties, when the moloch genius of applied science seemed destined to eliminate hawks in the civilised world (this particular flair doesn't abate either, one has only to listen to international statesmen, those wall-eyed souls left behind by our grunt-and-growl predecessors who snuffled around on the forest floor), all we could do was argue about possibilities, e.g. sterile eggs, the clutch stolen, replaced by painted hen's eggs, or the eggs had chilled as a consequence of disturbance and the cold late Spring. It was a very *secret* place, that tucked-back eyrie high above the steep scree down to the water's edge.

I set out to find a watch-point from the rim of the escarpment, even while realising it was impracticable owing to the overhang above the nest-scrape. Right, my 'scope was fixed up about 300 yards from the buttress. I saw the tiercel fly out. Through the glass then, simply a crescent of darkness above the grassy mound. Squalls of rain came. Mumbling half-promises to myself, I collapsed my gear and trudged back to the layby.

Deceived by a spasm of mid-day sunshine, I returned to our spot down below by the forestry fence. For the next three hours I crawled under and out of the dripping sitkas, trying to keep my body dry. Cold slashing rain intrinsic to hinterland Wales. Aye, 22nd May and it felt like the end of November. I did witness the tiercel sparring with the six ravens, four youngsters flying with the parent birds, and I watched the falcon crabbing out to the front of the grassy mound, turn around and disappear inside the small cavern. Beaten by the downpour though, I went home again.

23rd May promised fine weather, blue sky and healthy white clouds, so I clocked mileage to watch another eyrie in Powys. We were a few hundred yards apart when I saw the warden, suspicion prickling, until I recognised him behind his guru's beard and cavalier locks. We talked about peregrines. The single eyas was three weeks old. Negligently soaring, the falcon wove to and fro above the crags. Her primaries were ragged, fingered like a buzzard's, and she had a feather missing left of centre in her tail. I pegged across the moorland, canting sideways and slightly forward under the weight of binoculars, 'scope, tripod, packed coat and leggings, sandwiches and flask of coffee. A pipit feigned injury, scrabbling through the rust of last year's bracken. Twenty paces away from her four eggs, I propped a marker stone. For three seasons Allan and I marked pipits' nests on the moorland. They were always robbed by crows, ravens, magpies, weasels, stoats or foxes.

The eyas stood witchy-faced on the edge of the wide ledge. It had a top-knot of down, downy ridges on its long wings, thicker down on its belly, rump and tarsus. Infant raw-bird-meat eater . . . I set up the 'scope beneath a wind-ovalled hawthorn about 350 yards from the eyrie, and rolled a cigarette, my left eye staring at the chick. Warmth oozed into the afternoon. The falcon went in at 1.45 p.m. Her matt black lobes are very broad, accentuating the dullish yellow of her cere. Between attempts to brood the eyas she came out on the ledge, glared to left and right, tried again to squat over the youngster but it resisted, fidgeting, jostling

around her, while the big bird remained perfectly composed in the apparently timeless way of parenthood. I crept the 40X lens across, up and down, searching the great upflung cirque for the tiercel. All around the isolated hawthorn, cock whinchats were warbling from pinnacles of bracken, their wings and tails ceaselessly flirting. Pipits rose and descended in ecstasy—*wrong:* pipithood has no connection with poesy. When I thought I'd found the tiercel, delusion, wishful thinking, he came purling over the top and the falcon screamed. He left a blackish moorhen-size carcass on the outer rim of the ledge. The falcon lugged in the prey with her left foot, her head went up and down, scrupulous, feeding her chick for seven minutes, delicately, her carnal valency blocked off. Then she lowered herself sideways, only her head and throat showing. The eyas came out to the brink, it shuffled around the falcon, it wobbled out again, reversed, teetered and muted over the edge. Presently it snuggled beside the sitting bird.

At 2.40 p.m. a teenage couple strolled below the crags, the dawdling entrancement of lovers, pausing to embrace, nuzzle, breathe each other's breath. The falcon moved forward to watch them for a few minutes, realised they were harmless and returned to her sideways position. The chick had scuttled to the shadowed interior of the overhang.

The eyrie is about 10 feet above last year's site, set back at least a yard beneath the overhang, less exposed it seemed, although the reasoning of God's image is not that of peregrines. It was certainly easier for observation, better angled to direct sunlight. A clear atmosphere and sunlight are the hawk-watcher's coordinates. The warden feared a raid. Cunning, knowledgeable falconers are more dangerous to peregrines than yobbo criminals, and yet there is something antic, something lunatic about protecting rare species with barbed wire. I waited for a final sighting of the birds. Shortly after 3 o'clock the falcon flew towards a distant saddleback mountain. Hunting flight, I thought. She turned when only a fleck in my binoculars, and came back to the eyrie. Exercise, I thought. She was in moult too. Olympian fitness or death; peregrines have no alternative.

24th May. Sun glare above the escarpment, deep purple romanticising the buttresses and gullies. Our peregrines are either absent or comatose. A passing cloud gave me minutes to locate the tiercel perched below the eyrie. Returning to the road, I saw a fox coming sniff-sniff-sniff from a dry culvert. Vixen feeding cubs by the look of her scraggly fur and unkempt brush. Low to the ground, she went straight up the hillside.

For two days weathermen on T.V. smiled apologies. Mist and rain persisted, feeding the conifers. On Whit Monday we had the company of a retired G.P. and his wife. By now we felt convinced the eggs were either sterile or addled from chilling. For three and a half hours nothing happened at all. Skitters of rain, grey sky like a threadbare Army blanket, the kestrels coming and going, monotonous ring-ouzels, chattering magpies, the fretful redstarts, and thin, needling songs of goldcrests stitching through the sitkas. Our guests were patient peregrine-watchers. We tried to explain the extended duration of nest-reliefs. We drank coffee and ate sandwiches, altogether lugubrious, picnicking in drizzle, and hoping, against the evidence, to see the tiercel bringing in a kill for his brood. The doctor's wife had prepared crusty little bread rolls lined with pâté, each separately wrapped in foil. They were really serene, dignified, a gentle couple, incapable of the banal profanity which the Celt of rugby, soccer and boxing uses to backbone ideas and faith. Allan went home; he had a family commitment. A statutory nest-relief took place at 2.25 p.m. After a few minutes of ruffling and limbering on her tufted perch, the falcon flew over the mountain top.

"You haven't actually seen prey being carried to the eyrie?" inquired the doctor.

"Not once," I said. "That's what we're waiting for."

From under the hood of his jacket came, "Hm."

His wife looked perplexed, clutching her mittened hands under her armpits.

Two hours later the falcon swung empty-taloned above the reservoir. She threw down to the right, away from us, flapped in close to the buttress, narrowed her wings for the cleaving upward skim, and landed outside the scrape. The out-going tiercel flew south.

It rained all day on 28th May. Next morning the falcon hekked as I juggled the tripod's third leg. A crow pelted across the horizon. Hillside gutters foamed white torrents. Good light illuminated the escarpment. But came mordant necessity, a raging post-beer stomach, crucial mis-timing of bowelrun and bird. Afterwards I turned my 'scope on the kestrels.

The peregrines are absent for longer periods now. At 11.40 a.m. the tiercel arrived. He perched outside the scrape, plunged fifty feet, climbed as if sprung on elastic, and disappeared over the lowland conifers. I heard the falcon rasping quiet, prolonged whines in the eyrie. She tumbled out, down-slipping to scree level, flick-winged, ghostly grey over the darker stones.

How *twp** are peregrines? I wondered.

Nine immature herring gulls came from a rubbish-dump beyond the conifered common. They circled above the eyrie without reaction from the peregrines.

Rain swamped Wales again the following day. Until noon on 31st May, swirling mist saturated the escarpment. The tiercel brought in a small, gory carcass; he fed from 11.55 a.m. to 12.10 p.m. I lost him soon afterwards. Rain teemed down. Three ranks in from the fence, I curled myself around the base of a Christmas-tree. He brought another kill at 3.42 p.m., called to his mate while flying past the buttress, and waited for her on his flat look-out rock. Surgically exact, he unhooked himself from the half-plumed pigeon. I saw the falcon collect the prey and carry it back to the eyrie. Doug had seen a mid-air food-pass during the previous day's foul weather. Confirmed at last, we thought; eyases at long last. With varied ditherings we shared this fantasy for another fortnight.

Next day's sunny afternoon was upset by a tyro peregrine-watcher who inflamed my less-than-ingrained righteousness. He was a skinny fellow with a round, sparsely-bearded chin and fashionable dago moustache. Dressed in a green windcheater, jeans and turned-down wellies, he approached from directly above the central buttress. For twenty minutes he sprawled at ease about 30 yards from the eyrie, avid as a monk behind his binoculars while the peregrines screeched grand delirium, hurling up and down while this young bloke squirmed his private pleasure. I yelled

*dull witted

at him until he discovered me tucked against the forestry fence. He pulled a 'scope and pod out of his rucksack. We goggled at each other. I waved him away. His resentment suggested bigger problems than having regard for peregrines. As I say, righteousness invoked by a bonehead. Peregrines are *never* watched from directly above.

Many anglers were on the reservoir, enjoying the first really warm day of the year. During his early-morning watch, Doug saw the falcon taking a pigeon. White feathers were scattered on shale above the buttress. I packed in at 4.30 p.m., the tiercel perched near the rowan, the falcon in the eyrie.

2nd June. Before midday Doug cursed (coal-face lingo—he's a colliery fireman) two misses by the tiercel on passing woodpigeons. These evidently commonplace events are threatening to topple Doug's true-blue passion for peregrines. Every day he yearns for apocalyptic excellence.

I saw the tiercel coming in from the north behind a flock of pigeons, his long stoop ineffectual, but he planed in at 4.35 p.m. with a blue checker locked to his undercarriage. When the checker was partly plumed, he carried it to the crevice behind his perch. There were many pigeons flying today, homers, woodpigeons and rock-doves. Magpies foraging on the tops came lobbing over the summit, wings closed for the swoop down to the trees. They looked like hurtling plumb-bobs.

Early morning fog prevented any observation on 3rd June. Paul and I shared a flask of tea, smoked, and exchanged yarns about phenomena as always. The escarpment was clear by 12.30 p.m. Both peregrines dived at the family party of ravens. Lofting higher above the water, they interwove circles like twin deities until the falcon returned to the nest. The tiercel perched, sunshine glorying his throat and breast. He glided slantwise across the rock face, careered up a gully, turned, lifting in the updraught and stroked away to the west.

Paul thinned cigarette smoke from between his lips.

The tiercel came bat-fluttery from the south, the weight of a light blue pigeon making him look bumbling. He plumed the pigeon in nine minutes and cached the carcass.

Said Paul, "Eyases in that scrape? Never. You, Allan and Doug, you've goofed, man."

"Okay," I said. "No angels about these days, so nobody knows what's up there."

We watched the kestrels carrying small crunched mammals and beetles to their squealing brood on the shelf behind the silver birch. Presently Doug appeared, marching his single-minded gait alongside the forestry fence. He invented the idea of climbing to have a close look at the young kestrels. Paul followed him, zig-zagging around rough scree from the sheepfold to the rocks. The parent birds were swinging loops high above the mountain. Doug reached a wide safe platform of turf below the birch tree, twenty feet of smooth rock between himself and the fledgling kestrels. He clowned blithely, offering mimes, tableaux of wing and leg flexing, glaring peregrines. Paul allowed himself a belly-laugh. Doug's carry-on contravened ornithology as a science.

More mountain fog the following day. I glimpsed a peregrine flashing down the face of a buttress, and that was all.

5th June revealed a simple natural law. One of the four young ravens was grounded on broken shale. Somehow this young raven threatened ORDER, at least the peregrines' version of order within their territory. For weeks we had seen the four youngsters flying with the parent birds. I watched the tiercel taking off from a perch above a gully at 8.50 a.m. He hammered down on the young raven, screaming, the raven squawking and rolling its head. Soon the falcon came out from her hidden scrape. She joined in the mobbing. The other five ravens were mesmeric, like motes of dust rising and falling above the horizon of the far mountain. The falcon swooped four times on the grounded raven before returning to the eyrie, but the tiercel maintained his harassment. After a great blaze of stooping and screaming, he perched above the gully, his back to the vale, sunshine paling the dark velvet of his shoulders and wings. He gawked over his shoulder like an owl, he searched the sky, spun around on his perch, jigged his head and again flung down on the young raven. His screams were like the tearing of timber in a gale. Scurrying on short flights, the raven slowly progressed around the escarpment. The parent birds made no attempt to protect the youngster. For two hours the tiercel persisted, nonchalantly sometimes, floating back to his perch or roving yellowy atmosphere high above the water. Every time the raven flew, I tried to detect what was wrong with the bird. It didn't appear to be injured, nonetheless it was doomed. The next day and thereafter, a family party of five ravens foraged inside the escarpment and over the top of the mountain. Two hours peering through binoculars ached my eyes. It was a prolonged draw all right, so, relax, I thought, each to each the case is proven. The female kestrel crouched on the ledge behind the birch tree. I lined the 'scope on her. She yawned like a tired old fireside crone, her tiny innocent budgie head shivered and her horn-coloured mandibles clicked.

At 12.5 p.m. seven lesser black-backed gulls mazed shifting circles in front of the eyrie. They brought in the tiercel to a perch lower down on the buttress. Fresh from bathing, he was loose-feathered, his feet, cere and orbital rings glinting, long wings held out slackly from his body. Preening, he hoiked up his rump, white throat bulging like a pouter pigeon. A gull yawed up near him, wailing alarm. Other gulls came wailing off the water. The tiercel shook himself. His plumage settled. Neatly compact, he turned on the narrow ledge, his tail hanging down. Beak to the rock, he kept still for thirty minutes. Now he flew to a higher perch beyond the eyrie. More preening, finishing off, teasing breast feathers through the tooth and notch of his bill, working under his wings, his rump; all the while he looked around, scrutineer and prince of his kingdom. I saw his head jogging forward three times, then he muted as if the excreta was bicycle-pumped from his system, and launched straight out into hunting flight. Gulls fell quiet. Magpies broke off chattering in the conifers. A wheatear ceased bobbing. On the apron of the dam, four lesser black-backed gulls looked like toy sultans.

The tiercel returned without a kill. I went home. My wife asked me if I'd prefer a salad. This single summer day had come like a blessing.

Tempted by news on a chancy *Falco peregrinus* grapevine, I drove to Powys on 7th June. 11.30 a.m. at the solitary hawthorn and the weather overcast. As I tinkered with the 'scope the tiercel landed outside the nest-scrape. The eyas whined, concealed, I assumed, under the overhang. For some minutes the tiercel gazed at his chick. The whining continued, a distinctly infantile, sustained version of the adults' creaking-iron scream. It was a messy eyrie, trampled, deckled with feathers and mutes. A cock redstart fluted out his broken chaffinch's song in the hawthorn above my head. To the left of the eyrie, the white gorget of a ring-ouzel polka-dotted shiny black rock. I found the eyas at 12.12 p.m. Until its head moved I saw only lichen and sombre stone. It was squatting eighteen inches above the overhang. I wondered if the eyrie was too sodden for the youngster.

Within half an hour three jet planes roared low over the moorland. They left wakes of noise, samplers of alpha/omega. When the eyas stood up I saw it was a thriving young peregrine. Furry skeins of off-white down on the lower parts of its dark brown wings, ridges of down tufting the head and behind the neck. Scrabbling back to the nest-ledge at 12.45 p.m., right out to the edge, head nodding as if ready for flight, the chick searched for the parent birds. After preening and more searching, the same high-pitched, insensate whining arose as the falcon brought in the remains of a kill. She soon abandoned trying to feed her chick. Dropping sharply away from the left-hand side of the eyrie, she flew low, snaked up vertically, tight to the rocks, swerved with profligate ease high and clear of the cirque, and beat away to the west over the mountain. The eyas came out to the edge. Its legs were boxed inside white pillows. Yanking at its rump, eleven puffs of down floated away in the fitful sunshine. I saw the youngster retching to cast a pellet, retching hard, its head sawing from side to side. It ran back under the overhang for half a minute. Returning to the edge, it strode about, flapping, wings raised high. Another cross-wise passing jet plane sent it scuttling back under the overhang, but it quickly re-appeared, head craning to watch a softly prukking raven flying up a chute of scree.

Gauze shimmered as the sun climbed. The falcon brought a thrush-size kill at 1.25 p.m. The eyas whined. Dragging the prey in her right foot, she tore off a piece of meat and gave it to the chick. The chick ran under the overhang. The falcon flew out over the moorland, watched by the eyas. Instead of feeding itself, the youngster worked furiously, exercising, legging around on the ledge, wings flailing until it sat down exhausted, reverting to lichen and dark stone.

I came away at 3.50 p.m. The adult peregrines were airborne, soaring after making passes at a buzzard.

A pencilled message from Doug lay on my doormat: "*Our male brought in kills at 9.00 a.m. and 1.5 p.m. Third kill brought in at 5.40 p.m. Second kill was a RED*

CHECKER eaten clean down to the ribs. First and third kills cached near his perch. LISTEN, WE'VE GOT TO INVESTIGATE WHAT'S IN THAT SCRAPE. AGREED?"

The following day Doug introduced another watcher to the escarpment, a sensible young man, member of the R.S.P.B. and employed in the Fire Service, therefore unafraid of heights. Our peregrines were absent for 5¾ hours. We began to think the falcon had deserted, taken to whoring, or been shot.

"She's definitely a goner," vowed Doug.

"The eggs are," I said. "They should have hatched out a fortnight ago."

"Certainly, at the very least!"

We held a conference in Doug's house. The Fire Service chap volunteered to shin down the buttress on a rope.

"Permission," Allan said, rigidly concerned about legality.

"With permission," confirmed Doug. "Well-aye, otherwise see, we'll land ourselves in the mire good and proper."

I suggested we kept watch for another week. If the falcon was missing, another female might come along and mate with our tiercel.

"All right, but it's spitting into the wind," Allan said. "We don't know enough, not yet." He vetoed climbing down to the eyrie. Too dangerous. We had no expertise, no equipment. The shale above the buttress was pitched like a church steeple. Allan claimed he wouldn't climb down the buttress for all the lucre due to Prince Charles as inheritor of Mighty Albion.

Allan himself, he earns his living as a foreman roofer.

We savoured some cold comfort on 9th June. Two early-evening sightings of the tiercel preceded the falcon dashing into the escarpment from the east at 8.5 p.m. She copped on the grassy mound, lowered herself and disappeared under the overhang. Neither bird brought a kill to the eyrie, but the falcon was alive, still incubating. Now we could calculate how long the birds were prepared to sit on lifeless eggs beyond the 28-33 days' incubation period.

Nest-relief on 10th June had a fussy Darby and Joan aspect. Muggy and overcast by 4.30 p.m., frustrating haze grained the escarpment. Today I had company, Jim from London, water-colourist extraordinary in his heyday. To me he's like a brother, to my grandchildren he's Uncle. Doused with insect-repellant, reconciled to good and bad times in the past, we sat against the fence under the conifer branches. The cock redstart was singing his opening phrase of chaffinch repertoire while his mate sat on eggs in the sheepfold wall. Thirty-five years exiled and adapted to pavements, Jim's feet were tender. He wriggled his toes in the cool grass. I comforted my knee joints with fire-grease. We smoked cigars and drank percolated coffee spiked with brandy. Nest-relief took place at 5.33 p.m., coinciding with a lucky break in the haze. The tiercel landed on the grassy mound. The falcon crept out. They touched beaks, a curiously uxorious nibbling at each other, rather tiredly, I thought. He waddled in, she rose to her tufted perch, scratched and tidied herself as usual, and flew over the top.

We watched a trapped ewe on a curved, whinberry-covered ledge. She grazed. Without raising her head, bleatings came from her.

"Will you tell the farmer?" asked Jim.

"When?" I said, yoked to a schoolboy conscience, running to warn hill farmers about ewes stranded on cliffs, one farmer in particular bawling me out of his yard, "Clear off! Don't come yere pesterin' me!" Genteel crap, all the ever-so-nice legends. Welsh hill farmers, *mostly*, are the vinegar of the earth. Their sons and daughters become humanised by leaving home to work in factories, collieries, hospitals, or for British Rail and local authorities. Besides, they're a dying breed, dispersed by technology and the Forestry Commission. "That sheep will crop that ledge down to the clay," I said, "or she'll climb up the way she climbed down. Or try jumping down, in which case she'll make food for ravens, crows, maggies and foxes."

"Cranky up behind the eyes you are, butty," said Jim.

Two days later the ewe had left the ledge. I searched below the rocks for a scragged carcass. She was somewhere inside the forestry, where I could hear her snorting like a wild-beast.

Monday 11th June, we spent seven chuffed hours in Powys, watching the rampaging eyas. The big black faced falcon with her frayed primaries and missing tail feather, gathered a mealie pigeon from the tiercel, talons to talons in mid-air out in front of the eyrie, the eyas whining high pitched to the harsher screaming of the parent birds. They screamed as if in combat. I had a snatched glimpse of Jim's gasping mouth between the butts of his palms while he held the binoculars. Flying slowly, tracking for alignment, the pigeon dangling, the tiercel hung momentarily fluttering above his mate as she hurtled upward, rolling from below to take the pigeon. Pale feathers whuffed from the lifeless mealie. The falcon veered away, carrying the pigeon to a ledge in the shadows. The eyas remained silent while she

plumed. Feeding lasted for eight minutes. The eyas slumped, its shoulders and folded wings the colour of a dryish purple grape. Jim gabbled amazement. We saw the tiercel landing on a high spur at the far corner of the cirque. The falcon flew towards the saddleback mountain until she disappeared.

"I feel humble," Jim said.

"Privileged too?" I said—perhaps I wanted an excuse for my own peregrine-watching mania.

"Sure," said Jim.

I said, "It's taken a long, long time for peregrines to become peregrines."

The eyas slept, buzz-flies sparking glints where the 2 o'clock sun sliced across the left-hand side of the eyrie.

"What I love most is the mystery of these birds," Jim said.

"Not having much of it ourselves," I said.

"I have felt it in my painting. Rare though, less often than when colours used to make me drunk."

"Rare," I said. "Aye, true."

Jim went back to his white-coat job in London the following morning.

Another droll Darby and Joan incident at 4.50 p.m. on 12th June. Having walked along the brow of the escarpment, I set up my telescope slightly above eye level and about 300 yards from the eyrie. A rocky outcrop provided good background cover. This had to be an experimental session. I was close to a signposted footpath, one of the innocuous poxes of Big Brother environmentalists who would convert jungled Africa into tidy bijou plots of especial interest. Twiddling the magnification up to 40x, again I failed to penetrate the darkness inside the grassy mound. Suddenly, flaring into my surprised left eye, complaisant as doves, the falcon and tiercel appeared side by side as if consoling each other. They flew out. I couldn't help laughing in my throat. Beyond, beyond, the notion of two peregrines squatting in the eyrie. Still, how do they come to terms with a clutch of infertile eggs? Are they psychosomatically wounded, bereft, temporarily insane? It's easier to understand the instinct to lay another clutch of eggs when the first clutch is stolen. Peregrines are far-ranging travellers by definition, but they have a proven attachment to nesting territories.

14th June was cool and showery. I drove to Powys. Wearing Winter clothes, I stumped across the moorland. The falcon watched me from the soiled ledge outside the eyrie. At 12.38 p.m. she rose above the cirque, climbed until she was skylark-size and went down towards the north in three long swoops, each descent slanting thirty degrees across my line of vision, the first and second swoops ending on uptilted curves written on bleak blue, wind-shredded with streaks of white cloud.

I located the eyas blended to rootlets and rock a few feet above the nest. At 1.5 p.m. the tiercel brought in a small carcass. The eyas leapt down, grabbed the prey and raced back under the overhang. Bigger than the tiercel at close quarters, I gave her the ♀ symbol in my notebook. While the youngster fed herself, the tiercel perched on his high look-out spur. The falcon eyas came ploughing forward at 1.14 p.m. for a bout of growing-up. She wasn't ready to fly yet, but her time was near. Facing west, talons hooked into the turf, she piked into the wind, the hard sculling flight action of an adult peregrine. Tiring, she let her wings droop. She looked clear of nestling down apart from some faint traces of fluffiness around her rump.

Two hours later I met the retired G.P. He confirmed the eyas would soon take wing. There were rumours of an attempt to steal the youngster. The bearded warden had spent the previous dawn and dusk on watch. I mentioned the certain failure of our pair in the escarpment. Familiar with sicknesses, injuries, births and deaths, the old gent typified the contained quietism of his profession.

"They'll come back next year," he promised. A tall, heavy man, he tramped the cropped turf, waded through bracken and rushes, beyond the hawthorn and over a hillock, his head floating in isolation along the green land. He followed a stream to a great upthrust of boulders, chaos come to standstill. Here he prepared himself, unflappable watcher drawn to the most absolute bird in the skies.

But we lack the warp and woof of congruence. The destruction of tormentil seeds in the gizzards of blue tits register as meaningless; the death of a dove or song-bird by the talons of a hawk makes our nape hairs sizzle. Blind to the flight of sparrows, we catch our breath at the sight of a humming-bird. Between archaeopteryx and the firecrest, contrasting shades by the countless million. Birds whiffle in the imagination like mobiles in the insured atmospheres of museums. Aeons of babel separate us from lost time out of mind in Rhode Island Reds and Yorkshire Rollers. We have shambled from the primeval slurry like sleep-walkers.

I drove to the escarpment. In passing I spied a quick glance at the brooding redstart in the wall of the sheep-fold. The young kestrels were squealing. I saw the tiercel sweeping in below the skyline. He came from the south, rose to his look-out ledge, climbed higher into anchor silhouette against eggshell blue sky, then he flew casually, braked, at the same moment stamped his feet, and continued flying over the mountain. At 4.35 p.m. the falcon crouched into the darkness of her nesting-scrape. I heard soft, low-pitched peregrine screams. Using full magnification, I identified a shivering dandelion seed on the grassy mound where the birds landed. I suspected it might be down off a chick. Indeed to God, the relentless idiocy of hope.

Back in the car, I counted out the days. The eggs were almost two months old.

Nest-reliefs ceased on 16th June. The 15th was cold, windy, low clouds dragging from the west. The female kestrel hung above the scree slope, carpels angled high, her outer primaries raked down. At 5.57 p.m. the tiercel copped on a perch above the far gully. Wings split over his back, he preened for seven minutes. He glared out, hekked a few times and peeled away to the north. He returned with a pigeon at 6.22 p.m. The pigeon's wings flapped in the roaring updraught. He faltered above two plucking stations. When he landed the left wing of the pigeon windmilled into his face. He couldn't hold down his prey. He tore a strip of flesh off the pigeon's breast, the white of his throat writhing around to the back of his head, then he lifted off again, seeking shelter. Six inches away from the rock face, he thrust himself out of the updraught, lurching sideways to a lower ledge with a thick frontal barrier of whinberry bushes. I couldn't see him.

The weather changed overnight. Sightseers rowdied in the layby on the mountain road, licking icecream and watching the hang-gliders. Family parties paraded the pathway above the escarpment. Fortunately the path bends away to a forestry road. I waited below the path in a hollow of rushes and dry-slimed stones, 'scope focussed on the mound outside the nest-scrape. Everything quiet, no sign of the peregrines. Four youths climbed the far mountain; they rolled stones down into conifers below the dam wall. The male kestrel came lobbing up to my eye level. Ten yards away, he yo-yoed up a couple of feet, lowered himself again, dropped his right wing and fell on edge as if skidding. The youths bawled inanities, their voices carrying across the water. The falcon landed outside the scrape, stayed there for three minutes, looking around. She padded over the grassy mound. My eyelids twitched as if slaves to chorea. I saw her *turning* her eggs! Not the actual *eggs*, simply her head lowered and shovelled aside, and she made fastidious slow-stepping movements while settling down, leaving just the crown of her head showing like a tiny sliver of mole-pelt. It was 5.58 p.m., radiant

clarity on the buttress. When the youths yelled, she raised her head to watch them. They ran pellmell down to the dam wall. But there was no peace for her. Two bragging boys and two girls (one carrying a transistor) left the signposted footpath to walk a narrow sheep-track 40 yards above the buttresses. She skimmed out, soared over the lowland conifers and flew east. At 6.50 p.m. the tiercel came in. He incubated for four minutes, completely hidden, then he left, speeding off in the same direction as his mate.

My final extensive session at the escarpment took place on Sunday, 17th June, a warm afternoon with strato-cumulus breaking slowly at high altitude. The falcon was in the eyrie. Somehow I sensed anti-climax. Anglers shouted down below as if half a dozen Christs were walking on the water. For a long while the falcon stood at the back of the mound, looking out, motion-less, as if stupefied by failure. Eventually she flew over the mountain. Talkative strollers were enjoying the scenery from the footpath, trustless hominids for whom the Forestry Commission has designated safe picnic sites. A lone pigeon flew above the water, U-turned out wide and beat away to the west at the far end. Haze veiled the escarpment. I heard the conversational, squeaky *whinnicking* of peregrines. I searched without finding them. They weren't at the eyrie. At 5.5 p.m. the rasping frou-frou of a raven's hard primaries close to my head. The raven stalled in terror, jerking wings, tail and head as if blasted. Soft peregrine screams sounded at 5.18 p.m., very subdued, but I couldn't penetrate the haze. A flock of homers winkled like coloured shards over the conifers. The haze thickened. I stayed, listening for peregrines until dusk.

The 18th and 19th were perfect summer days. Coming off his regular night-shift, Doug's morning sessions were blank. The afternoons were fiascos, deep purple shrouding the rocks. Swifts dashed as if crazy-clockworked, gape-mouthed, harvesting boluses of insects. A small turd spotted the sleeve of my jacket. The male kestrel zipped screeching around the sailing jumbo of a buzzard. Later he swooped down on two

magpies perched in a rowan. He repeated his assault on another two magpies and a crow, quick, shortie falcon swoops less the menace and force of a peregrine. The corvids were too near the nesting shelf behind the silver birch.

The prowling sun brought dabs and licks of pea green light to peripheral foliage of rowans thrusting from the base of the rocks.

We failed to see or hear peregrines.

20th June, 7.30 a.m., a tranquil morning presaging afternoon heat. I found a dead badger on the mountain road. A mature boar. Almost 2,000 feet above sea level, no badger sett within a radius of twenty-five miles—I had no idea where he came from. Some skin scraped off his lower lip, otherwise there were no visible wounds on the animal.

The eyrie was deserted. Heat pulsed from the earth by 11 a.m. Half a mile away on the far mountain, the five ravens congenially palavered among themselves.

Doug was thoroughly disheartened by now, Allan more clinical, itemising all we knew about the peregrines and their failure to breed. Doug gave out grunts and sighs.

Facing sunrise at 4.30 a.m. on 22nd June, with heavy dew washing my boots, I walked around the escarpment. Heels digging in, I groped only part of the way down the steep clay and loose shale above the eyrie buttress. Here I tasted copper. I smelled dissolution, all my quick years ending in pulped bones and meat. So I went home. A couple of weeks later, with permission to act for the R.S.P.B., take the eggs (if there were any) and have them collected for analysis, I voted with Allan against the young Fire Service bloke climbing down the buttress. Too dangerous without reliable gear.

Early in May 1980, rigmarole tittle-tattle about our escarpment peregrines filtered out via urgent letters and phone calls. But that's another chronicle, and highly manic one at that.

PEREGRINE WATCHING: 1982

Peregrines are seldom absent for long spells from Cerrig Fawr and Cerrig Fach. These are fictive place names for obvious reasons. Searching for roosting peregrines on cliffs in Winter requires experience. The birds are inconspicuous. When holding territory in early Spring they invariably (not *always*) declare themselves, their white throats visible from a mile away through a decent telescope. In particular the tiercel's pristine as a dude's silk cravat against dark rock. When roosting outside the breeding season they perch under ledges, facing the rock or sideways, sometimes partly hidden by heather or whinberry. After rearing their brood, adult peregrines often roost and hunt some miles from the nesting area. Young birds occupy cliffs near the eyrie where they were reared until early October. They appear to depart of their own accord.

Finding a pair holding new territory at the end of February makes me grin with renewed relish. Having seen singles and pairs in severe weather, streamers and rivulets gleaming solid ice between the buttresses, I'm convinced peregrines are absent only when shortage of food takes them from Cerrig Fawr and Cerrig Fach. They are rarely absent from Fach for fourteen days in sequence. Cerrig Fawr is higher, a cardigan, scarf and gloves colder. Fach's buttresses are sheltered, more thickly vegetated, and nearer to reliable food supplies: domestic pigeons. I am old enough to remember the annual shooting of peregrines by or on behalf of pigeon fanciers. Shotgun law and greater affluence have virtually ended the vendetta. Falconers and egg collectors are now the menace. In 1983 the Cerrig Fach falcon was incubating on 19th March, phenomenally early, but the clutch was taken at dawn on 27th March. I kept watch later that same day. The birds were bewildered, visiting the empty scrape, calling, scurrying flights within the cirque, calling and calling. The same thing happened in '81 and '82, confirming the loco greed of egg collectors or some would-be falconer(s).

However, this record concerns the Cerrig Fawr peregrines. There were stinging sleet showers on 17th March 1982, five showers succeeded by washed clarity. From the hillside outside the cirque, I watched the peregrines flinging down on a low-flying raven. A tempest of ultimately harmless aggression. Breaking away, the falcon perched on a far-end buttress. Her mate raged jerkily above the raven, stamping his feet like a bull, then as if disgusted he flew screaming away over the top of Cerrig Fawr. The raven went planing, shiny as ebony, winkled up a gully and twitched beautifully out of the wind to the tucked-under nest where the female was incubating. She reached up to take food from his pouch. Ravens warrant respect. Their nest sites are usually safe from storms and predators. What a daft shibboleth, though, keeping wing-clipped ravens

in the Tower of London. How odious the trappings of Britannia, of medalled, ruffed and gartered seniles queueing up as if for divine elixir from her leathery dugs.

Leaving Cerrig Fawr, I walked outside a forestry fence for about two miles. Two miles of peat, clay and struggling moss, all the turf destroyed by paraquat twenty years ago. Six teal, four ducks and two drakes flurried down to a dug-out pond inside the forestry fence. Faint peregrine screams came from the cirque. Pricking sleet chilled my face. I would like to have seen a courtship flight, the stark exultation, halleluiah to their ascent from reptiles.

25th March: A bright Spring morning. Quiet, continuous wailings from the peregrines, raspiness ending on gaspy whisper, easily missed unless one's ear is attuned. These low calls precede copulation. The falcon crouched on a spur above a split waterfall of ivy. Holding herself horizontal, her beak gaped, softly calling. Find the tiercel! He flew across my glass, skimming edgewise, levelled and simultaneously braked above the ready falcon. Pretentious, trying to differentiate between roosters/hens and tiercels/falcons about sexual ecstasy. After copulation she fluffed out her plumage like a waterlogged tawny owl, dropped away from the spur and swooped up to the lateral break in the ivy. She waddled out of sight, soon reappeared and preened nonstop for fifteen minutes. The tiercel climbed in narrow-ended ovals above the cirque. When he stretched into hunting flight, he unspun down to a black dot, vanishing in eight seconds.

Relying more on instinct than second-sight or evidence, I decided they were making a new scrape at the break in the drape of ivy. Two days later, my legs and trunk lodged in a niche among boulders at the base of the cirque, I again saw the falcon briefly disappear behind the ivy. She shuffled out by degrees, rolled her head for some deliberate scratching, and flew to a rowan lower down on the buttress, where she stayed for over an hour. Peregrines are prone to 'hang about' prior to incubation. They have a tick-over dynamism millennias removed from what we regard as patience.

I watched the ravens feeding their young. Birds are coming into song, a ring ouzel, springy-legged wheatears, two far-off missel thrushes, broken trills from skylarks and spastic chittering from a pair of kestrels.

Misty pillars of sleet went spindling across the lower marshland. Late afternoon brought ceaseless wind soughing from the north. I packed my 'scope and tripod. Snow boiled down the end gully as I climbed to the top. At 2,000 feet just driving snow, familiar enough to anyone fixated with watching peregrines in the wild. Peregrines on the fist are like pensioned revolutionaries. And urban falconers, true as true, have the fatuous arrogance of successful serfs.

1st April: Ripples of snow crisping on the tops. At noon a single peregrine left the cirque, too fast and far away for me to say falcon or tiercel. Nothing else for two hours. Young ravens are defaecating over the rim of the nest. The kestrels bombard stone-grey skylight above the left-hand side of Cerrig Fawr. Thin rain bleared the afternoon. I cased my glasses and quit the watch.

5th April: Drizzle threatened as I poked straight

across the mile of tussocky molinia. Skylarks throbbing in the upper fog. The falcon was a yard clear of the ivy as my head showed above the buttress. I hurried away to the open hillside. Too early yet for this Cerrig Fawr pair to start incubating, but there were eggs in the scrape. She screamed down on a raven, the big hard corvid flipping aside and stolidly winging to its nest. Ravens and peregrines shared Cerrig Fawr when Wales was a shanks' pony nation. Ravens know more about peregrines than we do. Way out over the vale, two mewling buzzards sailed into mist, the same thickening mist sweeping rapidly across the buttresses. A ring-ouzel continued piping. Somewhere above the middle of the cirque, a peregrine screamed. Silence then, the driving mist hissing like a punctured leviathan. It was time to leave.

11th April: Sunny Easter Sunday, fathers and mothers stepping out of cars at the roadside, trooping their children and family dogs.

10.30 a.m. at Cerrig Fawr, the falcon on a turfed ledge, pluming and tearing strips of meat off a light-blue pigeon. Twenty-five minutes later she stropped her beak, a cobby whip-hand bird, fine dark grey barring engraved across her breast. She sprang forward, bandy-legged, instantly clenching her long toes. Tucked rearward, her balled feet hung like grenades. At 11.45 a.m. she returned screaming, chasing a stray female peregrine. The tiercel bowled out from behind the ivy. His mate plunged down into the cirque, stiff-winged, swept up to land on the patch of ivy roots and grass outside the scrape. As she squatted on her eggs, her right eye and half her forehead were visible. About an hour later the stray falcon reappeared, perching on a low rock shelf outside the cirque. I tracked my 'scope on her. Immature female. The tiercel returned with a plucked carcass. The stray took off, beating fast out over the vale. I watched the hungry tiercel cramming pale meat down his gullet. Afterwards he stood sentinel on a buttress adjacent to the eyrie. In a month's time, give or take a few days either way, these Cerrig Fawr peregrines would be feeding chicks.

12th April: 6.15 a.m., in time to see the tiercel bringing in a pigeon white as Picasso's dove of peace. Watched by the incubating falcon, he jerked out primaries, secondaries, tail feathers and swirling wads of breast feathers. He left it for her. After feeding for only a few minutes she flew with the carcass, screaming around inside the cirque. The tiercel winged back over the top, and she carried the carcass up a gully alongside the eyrie buttress.

Query, and not for the first time: who releases homers so early in the morning? Flocks of racing-pigeons are commonly seen after 7.30 a.m. and at various times during the afternoon. They follow high-ground contours, swishing along the brim of a hill, basin or quarry. Centuries of domesticity have left homers with the feckless fealty of trollops and gigolos.

The falcon left the gully. She landed outside the scrape. She looked down at me, pygmied among boulders. Through the 'scope I watched her settle her brood patch on the eggs, a melting rocking-wriggle. Again her right eye gazed unblinking. She was whole, given, wrapped in the sentience of ages. Slowly as a beggar I left Cerrig Fawr without disturbing her.

15th April: Falcon came back to the eyrie after three lads and three girls had walked around the brow. The tiercel arrived silently. He perched on a jutting rock below the eyrie, stayed there for almost two hours, then he lifted out, wheeling, soaring in sunshine. When he copped outside the scrape, the falcon slid forward through hanging strands of ivy. He incubated with his tail cocked up in shadow. The falcon slashed like a mirage, strange as a winged fish, past the buttresses, half-rolled, splaying her wings as she rose to open sky. She went away, threading into the south-westerly breeze until I lost her against conifers darkly blanketing a mountain several miles away.

18th April: 6.50 a.m. At 7 o'clock the tiercel brought in a red checker pigeon. He had already torn out the pigeon's wings. The falcon stood on the eyrie ledge. He finished pluming on stony clay just beyond her. As he carried the carcass to the ivied buttress, she uncoiled two great scything parabolas, rising below him, rolling over on her back, screeching, both birds screeching, the sagging carcass passing from talons to talons. Seldom witnessed in a season's watching, this aerial food-pass is usually a clamorous event. More often it happens when young are proving themselves on the wing, taking prey from the parent birds.

The falcon's meal was interrupted by the high-flying immature female stray, careering down the sky in elongated woodpecker-style flight, to perch on a near-side rock shelf. I saw the tawny streaking of her chest; by next Autumn she will moult into mature plumage and be capable of procreation the following Spring. Seconds fizzled away, the falcons watching each other. The tiercel came searing over the top, aimed himself at the stray falcon, and away she climbed, heading out, evading the tiercel. They quickly specked to nothing at all against light blue, dry-weather sky. I flung a mouthful of habit-swearing at them, at myself of course. When peregrines are radio crackles or blips on radar screens, the same curses will apply. Certainly we'll have more knowledge about the birds, in *absentia* for sure. Dogged sons of Adam forever gnawing at the apple.

After feeding, the falcon returned to her eggs. Seventy minutes later the tiercel came over the top for a stint of incubating.

20th April: Shortish mid-afternoon visit. Sun glare crowning the cirque. Buttresses shadowed. Thirty homers streaming like rainbow splinters against dull yellowy grass on the outer flank of Cerrig Fawr. The high hills are lush green for only six or seven weeks in Summer. Below the scree, a cock stonechat flicked on a bracken stalk. Farther away, old gnarled alders clumped each side of a brook where small, healthy trout have spawned since before the invention of the wheel. Willow warblers are in full song. Less insistent, the songs of redstarts and pied flycatchers.

The sitting tiercel faced inward. I saw the abraded tips of his tail feathers. The falcon stood on the mossed, horizontal branch of a riven oak tree. Perched on one leg, she sagged heavy-bellied. I wondered why birds rest on one leg. Birds and those lanky Dinka herdsmen.

28th April: Dry and sunny, unchanged for a fortnight now. Tramping conscientiously to Cerrig Fawr, I smelled peat smoke. Far away across the tops, a lop-sided square mile of young conifers was destroyed.

Here and there in the black welter, whiffs of smoke rose from peat smouldering six feet below the surface, peat laid down long ago, over a span of 65 million years—figures learned from a blackboard, Extra Mural classes, the Professor of Geology stepping aside, rubbing chalk off his fingers, cocksure of his exposition. Stationary prayer wheel, that man. Flat on my back under pouring skylarks, I chewed on his indigestible aeons. Education, I thought. Prescribed education, guaranteed to scar. I felt lightly scarred. Turning over on my elbows, I watched two crows prodding near a recurring pencil of peat smoke. Millions of insects had baked in the forest fire. The Forestry Commission offends ordinary common-sense, despite annual PR stunts. Like righteous gangsters they make enemies in the gospel name of Economics. Authority, power—inexorable as our exit from the womb and our end in dust.

I climbed down the right-hand side of the cirque. At 2.50 p.m. the tiercel flew up to a rowan in the gully alongside the eyrie. He stood motionless for two hours. Charcoal shadow concealed the sitting falcon. I screwed the magnification on my 'scope down to x15. She remained hidden, a presence, sealed as an oil painting grimed by fumes of cooking fat, candles and tobacco.

I heard myself sniffing like a troglodyte. Tangy traces of peat smoke in the air. Two sandwiches later, the tiercel made wing-tip-fluttering patrols inside the bowl of Cerrig Fawr. He was scrutinising me, pimping alien snagged among boulders, then he snaked up into shadow. As he landed outside the scrape the falcon slipped off her eggs. She tacked into the meagre breeze, reaching soaring flight when she was the size of an eyebrow, cramping to arrow-head shape as she poured away down the sky, falling into a dark land-mass far out across the vale, and I felt like a clodhopper.

2nd May: 7.45 a.m., overcast, the ravens active, their deep *prukk prukk* calls resounding as if the rocks were transmitting on HF. The food-carrying corvids never intrude into peregrine territory. Last Spring I heard two new sounds from ravens. KERLUPP repeated at long intervals, and from another bird perched in a conifer, bursts of rapid lapping noise identical to the amplified rippling of pages in a thick, heavy book. The remotely quiet "dead phone" BRRRT is another uncanny raven communication.

There are three fresh pluckings on ledges each side of the ivy-draped buttress. The falcon is incubating. Watching her, I saw the nictating membrane sliding down over her right eye, eerily glaucous, lizardly when viewed through a telescope, like a taunt to my own straining left eye. I scanned look-out perches, searching for the tiercel. No sign of him, so I settled on my 10″ x 10″ x 2″ piece of Dunlopillo (hoary peregrine-watcher's accessory after rainproof clothing, glasses, 'scope, tripod and victuals) to wait for his arrival. I heard the call notes of a cock reed-bunting among rushes down below the dry moorland, and lower down two cock tree-pipits claimed territories on the fringe of the alders. A couple of miles north of Cerrig Fawr, traffic swarms like seed-spill on a roundabout bigger than a football field. I couldn't see the roundabout from my nook below the buttresses.

The tiercel copped in after two hours. He had to wait on the ledge outside the scrape for four minutes before the falcon allowed him to incubate. More often, nest-relief takes place in a matter of seconds. She sloped across to the far end, swung out with a sudden bout of aerial shivering (gulls shake themselves in flight after bathing in fresh water), and turned in again to a gaunt, lifeless rowan tree. The tiercel incubated sideways-on, only his crossed wingtips and uptilted tail visible. The falcon stood hump-shouldered in the tree. Half an hour later, when I came away, she was preening. The ravens were dropping to their nest from above, pitching on the sticks, followed by a vulturine bounce, then landing firmly.

5th May: 3.20 p.m. Single swallows are flighting low across the top, heading north, obedient as mankind rising up off all-fours before immortally screwing himself in blind alleys of cause and effect. As I climbed down the left-hand side of the cirque, bad weather arrived. Sleet and rain. I crouched inside my razzle-dazzle camouflaged coat for 45 minutes. Large snow-flakes ran like suds in the sleet. By naked eye I saw the tiercel shooting down off the eyrie buttress. He sheared through the downpour like an apparition. Grim hunting weather. Heavy rain obliterated the buttresses. I climbed the right-hand hillside out of Cerrig Fawr. My knee-joints were like broken marbles grinding under-and-over by the time I slammed the car door. A sub-marine effect, all Wales scuttled instead of prinked with May blossom and fecund with bare-limbed maidens.

7th May: With Fred R., ex-town-planner, peregrine aficionado since his workaday years in Cornwall. Pellucid morning, confirming the everlasting flux of mountain weather. We had some good watching from 7 a.m. until noon. The falcon fed on a cached carcass while her mate sat on the eggs. She perched above the nest for half an hour. When the tiercel came off he glided way out above the alder wood, climbing gradually, drawing away to the south. Forty minutes later he returned without a kill. The falcon joined him, likewise planing, spread-winged, the tips of their primaries cleanly outlined. As she drifted over the top another falcon came scudding, passing below the tiercel. Perhaps she was the Cerrig Fach falcon, travelling south to her eyrie seven map miles away. It's rather maniacal to *imagine* the vision of peregrines. The finest Leica camera is a Luddite contraption by comparison, consequently photography is for photographers. Image-addicts. Flick-worshippers.

The Cerrig Fach tiercel of 1980 remains memorable. Perched on a spur above the nest, he hekked angrily (even *angrily* falsifies, because the sounding-board of evolution had registered peregrine vernacular before we unscrambled the yowls and yammering which resulted in Genesis 1.28), the jogging of his head warning me of his take-off. First the down-swoop for impetus, followed by hard thrusting wingbeats until he reached level flight. On he went with sharp decisive strokes, out and out against swollen off-white clouds. My 10x binoculars failed to hold him. Time drained away. From blankness I found two black pinheads shooting from right to left as if computerised, increasing to same-size tiercels as they curved down a vast trajectory, their screams spilling faint as static. The intruder plunged below the skyline, and the Cerrig Fach tiercel poured into a long, serene swoop back to the cliff, flung up close to the rocks and landed on his perch. Camera that lot, I thought. Polish lens to capture

Cerrig Fach's tiercel performing his run-of-the-mill stuff.

Fred peered through the 'scope at the sitting falcon. "Fine Bird," he murmured, repeating, "Fine bird. Marvellous. Why in the name of God should anybody want to take their eggs"—it wasn't a question. He went on to tell me about Colonel Ryves, an elderly gent when he knew him, dangling his legs over a Cornish precipice, pointing out some ancestral eyrie, Fred and the Colonel's wife feeling sick for his safety.

Years ago I had a goat's insouciance for heights. Now I quake in my gut when squinting down a buttress. And old Fred, he's worse than me. We are redeemed by West German binoculars, telescopes and more freedom from clock-time.

10th May: 8.30 a.m., the falcon shuffling around on her eggs. At 9.50 a.m. she pecked and pulled at bits of earth and rootlets from the edge of the scrape. Normal titivating behaviour of an incubating peregrine. The tiercel squeezed out subdued whinings. He was on a new perch, his back to the vale, invisible until he moved, the R.A.F. blue of him blending with the bare rock. His whining rasped louder, ceasing abruptly when he flipped down to his stand opposite the nest. In profile he looked gorged, puff-breasted like a randy cock pigeon. The falcon came off. She levered awkward hops to nearby ledges. The tiercel planed across but as he landed to take over on the eggs she barged in past him. The tiercel whined softly. This familial wrangling ended quickly. She flew, dropping away to the base of the cirque, springing a J turn, copping on a lower near-side buttress, where peculiar radiance blanched the dark cloak of her upper plumage to spat-grey. She turned full-front, her right leg angled out, quivering, the intensity slightly toppling her. We were 100 yards and time-out-of-measure apart. She glared innate genius, the ultimate of her kind, quintessential as tigers and sharks.

The tiercel incubated for 80 minutes. Relieving him, the falcon sat tight until 3 o'clock, when the pair flew together for twenty minutes, careening and stooping above the cirque, the bonding instinct, bondage to their race.

Distant particulars of nesting peregrines accumulate from observation. Hunting instinct relates the watcher to the birds. Peregrines kill to live. The watcher glimpses from inside the comforting mask of his own ignorance. Raptors reared in aviaries are directly germane to Genesis, our having "dominion over" a primitive business currently pursued by adult adolescents. Given a few more thousand years of perseverance, their disciples might manufacture sausage-dog counterparts of *Falco peregrinus*, by which time the field craft and cunning of today's eyrie-robbers will be seen as eccentricity, history's supply-and-demand system of *naturals* lubricating scientific progress. Peregrines are destined not to be left alone.

13th May: 9.45 a.m., falcon and tiercel perched each side of the eyrie. They grated thin calls as I approached my *cwtch** down among the boulders. Before my 'scope was fixed up, she flew to the nest. She faced outward, a heavily-barred wodge of her breast showing beside the immaculate dark edge of her partly-folded wing.

*cosy corner

For too long I failed to think about her strange stance. She was *higher* in the scrape because she was on chicks, clarified fifty minutes later when she flew to a cache below the tiercel and carried a wingless, legless, fist-size lump of meat back to the eyrie. Her bulk prevented me seeing her feeding the chicks. Impossible anyhow, from my crib below the cirque. The chicks are a couple of days old. She fed them for fifteen minutes. Meanwhile the tiercel streaked away. He was clipping fast and far out when I saw another stray peregrine (a falcon) stooping at him. He climbed, maintaining height above the strapper until she disappeared around the mountain. Returning to his perch, he made three indecisive approaches before landing. Only indecisive in my eyes; the reason remains his, of course.

The falcon carried the carcass back to the cache in her beak. She settled over the chicks, brooding, facing inward. Shortly afterwards she fed them again for a few minutes, and carried the carcass away in her beak, by now tattered and gory, less than half its original size. The tiercel was simply a looker-on. Once he came off to drive away a crow crossing the lower bogland. The crow had pulled out of a fracas with a raven. The tiercel chased the crow, indicating the greater threat to his territory. Sheltered deep inside a rowan at the base of the rocks, the crow was still there, hoarsely croaking when I left at 1 o'clock. Frightened pigeons will stay perched for hours after escaping from a peregrine attack.

14th May: 5 a.m. at Cerrig Fawr with two R.S.P.B. climbers. I sat well back while Paul abseiled down the ivy-clad buttress to mark the eyases. There are two, and a single egg, probably infertile. The egg later disap-

peared, trampled by the growing chicks. I don't know how or when a falcon ceases to regard eggs as her own, either to be eaten or abandoned. Viewed at a nerve-wincing slant from the cliff top, the chicks are simply two white, downy blobs. Their eyes are partly open: they are less than four days old. While the ropes were quickly stowed away, the peregrines tacked and veered across the wind above the alder wood, the tiercel higher and farther out.

After we left Cerrig Fawr on 14th May, the young ravens flew. At last they weren't on my conscience. I could scout for another watch-point. Near the rim of the cirque I found the ideal place, a rock shelf slightly above eye level with the eyrie. No more Sherpa-slogging down to that knobbly spot among the big stones. No more reeling vision from sun-dazzle above the buttresses. Altogether easier on my bones too, with miles of open sky to watch the birds coming and going.

15th May: The ordinary Spring and benevolent early

Summer of '82, when I learned more about peregrines than from books. We are all nurtured on mixtures of experience and second-hand knowledge, a hotchpotch distilled and expressed as personal. Disregarding John Donne, every man/woman is an island to himself/herself, islands in transit between the imponderable coincidence of birth and the certainty of death. Of course we *share.* Cheapskate experiences and bearable truths are commonplace, the meal-tickets of professional explainers, organisation people, political leaders, theologians, lawyers. Yes, we share all right, the light upon our separate selves.

From a sure-bet beginning, for the past ten years I have shared some birdwatching experiences and conclusions with Allan. We were set snug against the high-level rock shelf at 9 a.m. It was panoramic. We didn't have to wiggle around on our rumps to follow events. The falcon squatted over her chicks, her mate stood on his favourite look-out perch, the projecting nib of rock about fifteen feet below the ivy. The four young ravens made sporadic flights, travelling across moorland between the scree and half a square mile of boggy watershed, where a spread hand of ever-running streams feed the brook through the alder wood. Skylarks shivered under the sun, endlessly trilling. When the peregrines are waiting on, patrolling in the west wind above the cirque, skylarks stay on the ground. The belling of a ring-ouzel went on and on, plangent, deceitfully wavering from gullies, buttresses and scree. We located his white bib in a dark slot of green-slimed rock.

The vigour of peregrines is demonstrated early in their lives. After a few days the Cerrig Fawr falcon stationed herself a foot or so away from her huddled chicks. Kills for the larder were left on ledges in a yawning gully alongside the eyrie buttress. She carried a plum-red carcass from the gully at 11.25 a.m., and fed the chicks for 25 minutes, concentrating on each chick until its waggling gape dropped. She hopped back, her left foot clutching the carcass.

The tiercel jogged his head, watching a snipe careening away from the oncoming young ravens. When he eventually took off, the tiercel flew along the southern flank of Cerrig Fawr, pierced the skyline, clipping and gliding clockwise gyres, cutting deeper south, away around a treeless mountain.

The falcon fed her chicks again at 2.10 p.m., frequently twisting her head so that the youngsters were fed upwards. I believe this feeding-pattern is imprinted on eyases. Youngsters from the same nest, when they are fledged and on the wing, go through the same motion with each other. Presumably this mimicry serves them when they are feeding their own broods as adult peregrines. Falcons are reputed to resist the tiercel tending to his chicks for the first 10-14 days, but last year (1981) I heard the Cerrig Fach falcon calling to her mate from the eyrie. He was perched with a full crop. The single chick was seven days old. After a while he went to brood the chick, creeping forward to it from the back of the scrape. The falcon went hunting for fifteen minutes. She came back with a starling which she plucked near the eyrie. The tiercel returned to his perch when she carried the carcass to the nest, and the chick was fed. She also fed herself off the starling.

We watched a magpie climbing like a tit up the tail-end of a grazing ewe, searching for ticks in the wool.

Allan said, "When the rams are let out in November, I've seen starlings feeding on them."

The magpie rode a few yards on the ewe's back, and flew down to the alder wood.

Leaving her chicks clumped together, the falcon tore the last pieces of meat off the skeletal remains. She dropped the blackened rib-box as she came off the ledge, a handy chew for a scavenging fox. There are utilitarian links in the ecological chain strung by breeding peregrines. I have watched chaffinches foraging on a massive old stick nest vacated by a female eyas only a few hours previously. Tits, warblers, stonechats, wheatears, sparrows, starlings and redstarts are supplied with nest-lining feathers from pluckings. Nourished by decades of droppings (from ravens and peregrines), maps of pale green algae on barren cliff faces are pointers to ancient breeding-sites. As with all raptors, peregrines batten on runt prey, on young birds, the singularly odd (cuckoos for example), inadequate, injured or diseased. White pigeons *seem* most vulnerable in a flock, but there are many more pluckings of dark blues, reds, checkers and mealies near peregrine eyries. While ravens are harassed time and time again by peregrines, they often share a cliff-face where there are alternative nesting-sites. Sometimes, however, ravens are driven to quit a site and the nest is taken over by peregrines. As for crows, when they attempt to nest near an eyrie, they are remorselessly attacked and killed. Obviously enough, wild peregrines do not trust crows, neither does the experienced falconer, conscious if not proud of the small fortune hooded on his fist.

My personal impressions at a cliff where peregrines are breeding are multifold. The birds dominate exclusively, spreading terror and hush. Prudently speaking, I become a fragmentary part of their lives. By the same token, the peregrine-watcher lacking a sense of awe might just as well spend his days selling sink-units or milling blanks for pennies. Of such are the kingdoms of democracy.

19th May: 9.30 a.m., warmish, rain due this afternoon. I missed a feed-time by minutes. The falcon lifted off with a carcass, one pink-fleshed leg hanging down. She replaced it in the larder gully. Flapping strenuously for the next ten minutes, the deep flexions of her wings reminiscent of a thornback ray whipping up clouds of sand, she cruised low above the rim of the cirque, then she copped on the ledge beside the chicks. Two hours went by. Once, as if blessed with "eyes in the back of her head", she swept out, deflecting two young ravens crossing Cerrig Fawr from end to end. Seconds later she returned to stand guard at the eyrie.

Shooting down from a grey sky, the tiercel came in with a breathy whoosh, slicked up the buttress and landed on his perch below the ivy. He screamed harsh and repetitive. The falcon remained unmoved.

One of the chicks staggered backwards to defecate against the rock behind the scrape. The youngsters are brawnier, coming into their second coat of down. Odder than mysticism, red wrinkled babies becoming tycoons and pianists and tomato-growers and film-stars, and these wobbly white creatures roving under heaven as peregrines.

The tiercel launched off his perch and turned sharply up into the larder gully. He was probably feeding. Presently the falcon walked forward, gripping sloping ivy roots at the edge of the ledge. She watched him, but

I couldn't see him. The domestic ways of peregrines have abrupt anachronisms, tempting but dangerous to label with human feelings and sense. Another fallacy comes from seeking to encompass peregrines in terms of diagrams, tables, irrevocable statistics fashionably arranged, presented as ornithological grammar, violating the living bird as a blinkered grammaticaster misses the poet. I regard peregrines as exemplars, not to be found in packs of histograms. Enthralment is seeing and hearing. A somewhat deviant event the following day reinforced my faith.

20th May: 4 p.m. The falcon stands eighteen inches away from her chicks, the tiercel below her on his perch. Lull for two and a half hours. Shortly before she fed the youngsters, he flew out and back in, wailing huskily low key as he landed. She fetched a plumed carcass from the larder. While the eyases were being fed, the tiercel screamed up at her. Absorbed by watching the falcon and the chicks, time lost importance, waffled away from me until the tenor of his screaming registered. It was high-pitched, the urgent,

crackling whining of a lusty, hungry eyas. Then he flew up to the nest-ledge. He attempted to pull the carcass from the falcon's talons with his beak. Twice he tried to wrench the kill from her. She backed off, wings flailing, silent, the tiercel still screaming. After the second attempt she fed herself for a few minutes. Again the tiercel flew up from his perch and grabbed the carcass with his beak. This time it was also in her beak. She released it. His screaming rang harsher, celebrant as he carried the carcass around a buttress. Now he was hidden from me. Silent as before, she left the chicks and perched in a tree overlooking the gully where he was feeding. Uselessly sympathetic, I thought, poor starving tiercel. The chicks were 9-10 days old.

Eight minutes later she returned to stand on the eyrie ledge. Straightaway the tiercel brought the remains back to the eyrie. She gobbled two small pieces of meat and continued feeding the chicks. And the tiercel, he swerved out, down and up to his perch on the buttress. Maybe this was a one-off incident, a wayward lapse in peregrine eugenics. Clichés about peregrine behaviour are the currency of pseudo-experts who shy away from Nature red in tooth and claw. For them it's all romance, benign romance coloured by bird-sanctuaries, R.S.P.B. reserves, bird-tables and tit-boxes, robin Christmas cards and lapel-badges.

For the next half an hour the falcon fed her brood, waiting compliantly for a raised gape from the collapsed eyases. Eventually she fed herself, ripping stringy pieces of meat off the pigeon (it had been a standard pigeon-size carcass) bones and finally dropping the bare ribs while winging across to a nearside buttress. She was now about 70 yards from me. Facing the eyrie, she picked her toes clean and preened through her belly feathers. She was still scratching and preening when I crouched over the top at 9 o'clock.

25th May: Bright 8 a.m. with roaring wallops of west wind, the falcon beating and hovering above the cirque. My eyeballs jiggled, unable to escape from countless ribbons of dead molinia flitting, whirling over the top and down the buttresses. I wrapped a lightweight poncho around my legs. The chicks are ghostly white this morning. Lowering skies make them look smudgy. They have learned how to whine, to galumph about and flap their stumpy wings, wings tinged with dark quill at the edges. From 8.30 a.m. to 8.50 a.m. they were fed on prey from the larder, a begrimed scrag of meat, left in the nest when the tiercel arrived empty-footed. He seemed full of rage, his screams forced into rabid chatter. She flew with him very briefly before returning to the eyrie ledge. By 11.5 a.m. I had lost track of the tiercel. At midday the falcon went over the top for twenty minutes. She stood by the chicks for five minutes and went off again. They were short of food. At such times peregrine-watchers are inclined to futile anxiety, puny frets of the earth-bound. The youngsters were surely hungry, only one skimpy meal since 8 a.m.

1 p.m., the falcon gazing at her chicks, then with the wind behind her she sliced away from my sight in the dark land-mass of the vale. Fifteen minutes later the tiercel left a small plumed carcass in the larder gully. He screamed a couple of times, his black head turning, looking for his mate as he flew out beyond the alder wood.

2 p.m., the tiercel again, swooping up into the gully. I think he fed before perching on his look-out spur below the ivy. He called ceaselessly from 2.40 to 2.55

p.m., when the falcon came in with a fresh, sizeable carcass and fed the chicks. Taking turns without squabbling, she pushed pale, raw meat into their gullets until their crops bulged out in front like side-by-side hen eggs.

Irregular creak-squeaks came from the riven oak, gusts rubbing two branches against rock and each other. Totally senseless trying to evaluate what human ears pick up in the nominal three score and ten of their owner. Every orifice contributing besides, swelling the delta of the mind. Hi yi towards the ocean. Nirvana of course, aye, never-nevered in bedrooms, bathrooms, lavatories, hallucinating at the breast and counting money.

Forgive us our prayer-makers.

28th May: Late evening visit with Allan. For two and a half hours we quietly chilled to the marrow. The chicks are thriving, tobacco-brown feathers unsheathing on their wings and tails. They flapped, they pecked at ivy twigs, between times they shat cleanly out of the eyrie.

Many grassed ledges in Cerrig Fawr are spattered with pluckings. Breast and belly feathers drift away in the winds, primary and tail feathers lie all-shapes, like the collages of schizophrenia.

Drear evening on a Welsh mountain, the falcon standing motionless. A pair of kestrels squealed around the heads of two ravens as they slugged raspily past a forked-lightning fissure where the kestrels are nesting on the right-hand corner of Cerrig Fawr.

Allan said, "Ravens were Odin's birds of omen."

Unnecessarily I said, "You sound like Henry Williamson at his worst, drivelling on about . . ."

"Odin-Woden . . . Look! Tiercel coming in at ten o'clock," said Allan.

We heard the dry whew of his dive into the cirque, saw him arrow upwards and land below the eyrie as if magnetised. After a while he hooked up his slackly bunched left foot into his belly feathers.

The chicks were fed after we came away. First and last light are prime hunting times.

29th May: 2.30 p.m., heat-haze in contrast to yesterday evening's gnawing cold. Rapid weather changes in the hills are prescribed in the manufacture of S.A.S. unmentionables and Duke of Edinburgh Award winners, innocents from the back streets with minds for bending. Today, down in the alder wood, Boy Scouts are camping. A whoopee (Yaroo!) combination of Top Twenty records and stylised adventure. No doubt most of the lads camping below Cerrig Fawr will remember the occasion for the rest of their lives. Two pairs of pied flycatchers and three pairs of redstarts are breeding in the wood. There are over 10,000,000 Boy Scouts in the world, all of them learning about self-sufficiency, valour, good deeds. Some will take on the charisma of politicians, civil servants, scientists, criminals. Most of them are destined for anonymous citizenship, tied to honest jobs, rearing kids, mowing the lawn, switching on the news, football and horses, saving for holidays, believing in neighbourliness, unforgiving towards turncoats, villains, and cherishing particular heroes.

Blurred inside the haze veiling Cerrig Fawr, the falcon fed her chicks. The rowdy campers had driven the tiercel elsewhere. The falcon flew across to the next buttress, dropping a bundle of bird-bones en route. She returned to the eyrie, spun around on the crouch in the scrape itself, just her eyes and forehead showing above the ledge. The chicks exercised, flailing, buffeting, and flopped. One clambered behind thick ivy-roots, the other hunched in gloom at the back of the falcon.

I held Lord Baden-Powell responsible for the loss of a clutch of pied flycatcher's eggs, at least, and a brood of grey wagtails.

30th May: The eyases are 21 days old, and fortunately the Boy Scouts are trailing away through the wood. Soon, the primordial state left over from the last Ice Age. Skylarks are excelsior this morning, carolling hosannas over the tops. Scoop-winged titlarks volplane down to the lower moorland. Territorial songs from wheatears (sophism for white-arse) occupying the scree, and always the monotonous, elusive piping of a ring-ouzel. A heron, probably a non-breeder, picked beetles, water-boatmen and tadpoles from a scummy bogpond no bigger than a billiard table. Throughout the seasons, herons have become more common since the Sixties, cleaner rivers marking the gradual demise

of King Coal in South Wales. The nearest heronry is 25 miles away, sustained by mass-produced rainbow trout in Welsh Water Authority reservoirs.

The eyases slept. Twice the tiercel came in without prey. At 12.15 p.m. the falcon fed her brood from the larder, the chicks watching her finishing pluming a bronzy blue and white pigeon, simply watching in silence, learning their inheritance. One of the chicks is smaller, a tiercel eyas. After the meal he left the scrape to hide behind the barrier of twisted ivy-roots. The falcon eyas pushed herself into the dark interior.

Heat flowed into the day. Bluebottle flies glistened on the pigeon carcass. The old bird gazed out over the vale, somnolent, heedless it seemed, disregarding a flock of twenty homers cascading down at the far end of the cirque and streaming around inside the great amphitheatre of buttresses. Blues, red checkers, grizzles and mealies, they swept by in pop-eyed concord, rising clear over the top.

Seeing the heron leap into squawking flight, I swivelled my telescope. A fox headed through the lank grass bordering the pond. Poised on three legs like a pointer, the fox watched the heron's prancy landing on one of the outermost alders, then the rusty brown shape rippled down a naked peat bank slanting away from the pond. Day-time foxes are rare until high Summer, when cubs of the year start hunting independently.

The female eyas stumbled across to the edge, reversed herself and muted, the sunshot excrement disintegrating like a broken necklace. The other chick followed suit. The old falcon ignored them. Far-off hekking prickled my eardrums, but the sky was bare. I expected to see the tiercel biting along under the blue. A missel-thrush churred in the alder wood, the rattling churring which accompanies attack. Gutsy birds. They have to be, building their straggly nests while trees are in bud.

The chicks worked, winging on the spot as it were. Later they would be leaping and flapping like dervishes.

Nine torrenting skylarks rang my senses as I stooged back across the summit. Spurred by utter incongruity, I daydreamed about my ancestors migrating to this part of Wales to hack and shovel coal five generations ago. In whatever scheme of things, I thought, we are as sand on the beach. From inside the car I watched a family of starlings rummaging on rubbish dumped at the roadside. Silicon-chip folk have the careless nous of fellahin. We trademark the earth with refuse. Brown young starlings trotted around the speckled parent birds like marionettes.

1st June: 9 a.m. guaranteed a hot day. The male eyas sheltered in his cranny behind the ivy roots. While the sun blazed on the eyrie, the falcon planted herself in front of the other, exposed chick. She was behaving instinctively, instinct rooted in extremities over geological time. Watching, I cultivated a smidgen of patience. Patience time-tabled to reward. At 12.15 p.m. shadow began sliding vertically across the falcon's back. Fifteen minutes later the shadow covered her. Without haste, she turned and sway-walked out to her usual stand on the ledge. The chicks roused, nibbled debris in the scrape; when they whined the falcon swept down and up to collect a carcass from the larder gully. It was a sun-dried, featureless lump of meat. She no longer twisted her head to feed the youngsters upwards. I regretted failing to note when she ceased presenting food in this manner.

Weeks later, when the eyases were strong on the wing, I saw the young male adopting the same pose, head twisted as he gently dibbled at the underside of his sister's bill.

The eyases slept in a heap. The falcon carried the prey back to the gully in her beak. Having searched the cirque for the tiercel, I assumed he was perched around the other side of a buttress. I felt my eyelids coming down. Concentration waned. I dozed, oblivious as a dog in front of the fire. Waking, I saw the falcon scratching the side of her head, a yellow toe digging like a sickle near her closed eye. Three crows foraged on the sheep-cropped moorland beyond the scree. Shimmering heat transfixed the green alder wood. Standstill flecks of light starred the brook. As the crows took off, a matt slate-blue phantom swooped, grabbed a dead auburn and white pigeon from tailings of scree directly below me, and carried it to the larder gully. It was 2.30 p.m., proving the tiercel had struck down and killed the pigeon at least five and a half hours earlier. He "remembered". Twenty minutes later he left the headless victim on the eyrie ledge. *Victim:* a typically erroneous noun when applied to raptors.

After feeding her chicks the falcon carried the carcass back to the gully. As I lowered my binoculars, I saw the female ring-ouzel leaving her nest.

When I arrived home, a tea-addicted neighbour woman predicted casually, "They'll find you out on the mountains when you're at your last gasp. Thank goodness none of your children follow in your footsteps."

5th June: Three days of grogginess, bone-aches and stomach-ruth, before this evening's visit with Allan. The heatwave continues. Eyases are feathering and fit. The male eyas has less down on his head and rump. He's more rumbustious. The old falcon supplies food according to demand. She held a gobbet of meat in her bill for six minutes. A few years ago I watched young sparrowhawks from a hide. There was a marked difference in the development of each chick. Invariably the female sparrowhawk fed the weakest, youngest chick first. Eventually they left the nest on the same morning, white down tufting like cottongrass on the head, mantle and rump of the last-hatched chick. Peregrine chicks do not receive preferential treatment.

The tiercel and falcon flew above the moorland for half an hour. Although this flight lacked the challenging stoops and frenzied screeching of courtship in late February and March, it was obviously binding. They were a pair. Most of the screaming came from the tiercel.

I spotted a sooty black, unringed feral pigeon on a buttress this side of the eyrie. Rigidly upright, with its neck stretched, the pigeon gawked at the peregrines. And then single pigeons careered madly over the top or came plummeting down the outer hillsides. Occasionally in twos and threes, the homers flung from all directions. They were in panic, disoriented, incapable of flocking. When the sooty feral took off, another pigeon arrived alongside. Streaking around the cirque, they skimmed low to the ground down to the alder wood. The peregrines wheeled, flung short stoops, flung up again, wheeling.

Allan said, "I suspect we missed seeing a kill."

Returning to the car, we found a fresh plucking on a sheeptrack. The pigeon's shrivelling tubes and intestines were spangled on tough new spikes of June molinia grass. Happening to glance back from a few hundred yards away, we saw a pair of magpies pulling at the dried intestines.

8th June: 9.00 a.m. This rare windless morning, a wispy-edged streak of fog burning away above the brook. The chicks preened desultorily, snippets of down fuzzing their beaks. I saw the tiercel on his look-out below the eyrie. The falcon was perched in a rowan, higher up and across the next gully. They flew together at 9.45 a.m. She soared without flapping for twenty minutes. The tiercel soared far out, beyond reach of my glasses, and he returned still soaring. He threw out bursts of screaming. At 10.05 a.m. he copped on his perch. The falcon soared. He screamed again before joining her. They planed wide arabesques, disappearing over the vale. She came back at 11.15 a.m., inflexibly soaring, unlike the wafting of a buzzard, and floated out of sight.

The male eyas is clear of down on his head. The falcon

eyas has light swatches of down on her wings, with tufts whiffling above the darkening velvet skullcap of her head. They slept. When the falcon reappeared below the skyline, they whined quietly. She soared, waiting on, drifting, drifting. I lost track of her.

The tiercel landed by the chicks. They gaped and whined at him. He soon left, exactly 30 seconds before the falcon crashed in with a pigeon carcass. She fed the male eyas for seventeen minutes. The female youngster staggered and flapped, gulped some dollops of meat from the old falcon and hid herself in shadow at the back of the scrape. The fullcropped tiercel eyas climbed behind the ivy roots. All the while, intermittent screams from the tiercel perched below on the buttress.

Absolved from natural enemies (except foxes), peregrines at the eyrie often set up a hullabaloo which can be heard a mountain away, prompting the knowing human ear to seek out, possess or destroy, ourselves being the best no-holds-barred predators in a history kicked by religions, wars, and the diagnosis of diseases. Glory and doomsdays proliferate.

The falcon dropped away, canting, straightening herself, up into the larder gully, leaving the carcass on the nest ledge. Less frequently now, the tiercel screamed on his perch. When the falcon flew from the gully she kept below the skyline. I lost her for a few minutes. Next she was bringing in another pigeon, a low-level snatch, delivered straight up into the gully. At 2.35 p.m. she skimmed around to the nest. The female eyas was fed to repletion. After ferrying the carcass back to the gully, the falcon stood on the sharply sloping outer edge of the eyrie.

A spell of equable doldrum in Cerrig Fawr, jarred by occasional screams from the tiercel. He took off an hour later. Both birds were airborne as I came away, the tiercel screaming. Raving garrulity seems to afflict peregrines. I can't find a consistent rationale for what comes off my own tongue, let alone the rise and fall of official spokesmen.

11th June: 2.00 p.m. As I dawdled across to the sheltered rock shelf, the tiercel flicked and veered farther away. He has no more reason to trust me than all the saints in stained glass. With his head tucked, the male eyas is sleeping out on the ledge where the old falcon normally stands guard. The other eyas sleeps recessed in shadow behind the ivy curtain. While watching the tiercel, I glimpsed the falcon winging in below him. She stalled outside the scrape before rounding into the larder gully. The tiercel stayed way out, criss-crossing above the alder wood. A jet plane roared over Cerrig Fawr like a Third World catastrophe. I saw the falcon's beak, eyes and forehead slide forward into view, hesitant, retreating again as the noise faded. The tiercel copped on his perch below the eyrie. He screamed on and off for 45 minutes. At 3.20 p.m. the falcon went hunting.

The chicks stood shoulder to shoulder. Dead-leaf brown vertical streaks on their breasts are prominent, the female more resembling her sibling now, with only wispy strands of down on her wings and head. I heard their crack-throated whining when the falcon came in, but she had nothing. Trundling apart, they tugged at old scraps of food on the ledge, merely clusters of skin and bones. The male eyas scuffed around, bones and dried membrane in his talons. Rearing backwards, pulling it with his beak, the papery skin split like silver birch bark.

The falcon flew up into the gully. She remained concealed for over an hour. The larder was bare. I harboured some more worthless worrying. The tiercel climbed, ringing up above the cirque. Empty sky everywhere. Seconds before he passed over the horizon, I saw him thinning into hunting flight. The falcon stayed in the gully.

Peregrines have, or seem to have in our terms, a saurian endowment for stillness, yet even in repose they embody wilderness made flesh. I would feel ashamed to flaunt a peregrine on my fist. Impossible to imagine an extension of these birds; the mind cringes, peeps out of its hole, chats to the postman about primroses, larkspur, having it off, interior decoration.

When the falcon dropped clear of the gully, she floated over to a grassy deck soiled by many pluckings. Whatever she heard or saw escaped me, because just then the tiercel came in at eye level, landed on the deck, bobbled to unclamp himself from a light blue pigeon, and left her to plume the bird. He flew to his perch below the eyrie. The falcon knew her mate was bringing in food. As always the chicks were fed in turn.

13th June: Early morning, thick fog rolling, interminably slow-rolling across the buttresses. Untrustworthy mountain weather. A falsetto-bawling farmer neuroticised his sheepdogs on the hummocky moorland between the scree and the boggy watershed. Hill farmers are weird left-overs from pre-internal-combustion engine days. E.E.C. funds are helping them fence vast tracts of mountain. Extremely effectual too (unless the peaceful yomper has a junior hacksaw in his pocket), mountain ranges captured by fencing contractors in a few weeks, and guaranteed to last twenty-five years. All

praises, the political tykes of the EEC. Like the Forestry Commission, they have the same long-headed dipsy-do as the builders of the Great Wall of China.

The farmer's yelping diminished as he went (probably on horseback) from right to left, where the hillside gradient waves steeply between transverse hollows of bog down to the huge roundabout. I sat with crossed ankles in fog for an hour, like a lost-cause Canute. I peeled a Common Market apple. The cock ring-ouzel, caterpillars writhing in his bill, pitched two yards away from my wellington boots. As he took off, his mate dashed below, dropping a faecal sac. They are feeding four half-fledged youngsters in a nest squashed between rock and a whinberry clump. Ring-ouzels are nervy Summer visitors. They chatter loud as blackbirds when flushed off the nest—a unique event. After being disturbed they will not carry food to their young until humans are fifty yards away.

Fog, fog. Time to go home.

14th June: Warm, clear mid-morning. Before raising my glasses I saw the empty eyrie. Panic stiffened my throat. Raging fear. Some unforgiveable waster had taken the chicks. Two buttresses beyond the nest ledge, the old falcon stood in a dead rowan. A creamy white pigeon feather sticking up from the crown of her head made her look silly. She cleaned between her toes, the feather bobbing. I was about to walk across to the ivied buttress when the tiercel came in. He screamed on the nest ledge for fifteen minutes. Fear crawled under my skin like rot. Sometimes the tiercel cocked his head around, more often he appeared to be screaming at his mate. Well, she'd gorged herself by the evidence of that clownish Redskin feather tacked with dried blood to her black head. Quaintly then, but immensely satisfying, one of the eyases came crabbing around a spur above the screaming tiercel. They were safe. The youngsters were footloose on the buttress. Eyases do not fly straight from the eyrie. In 1980 I watched a youngster scrabbling around on ledges for four days before it took wing.

The tiercel grasped a fresh, untouched carcass lying in the scrape and flew to a wide green ledge below the dead rowan. He kept up his screaming, encouraging the eyases to follow him. However, he had to take it back to the eyrie. The second eyas crept laterally across the ivy like a cat-burglar. It was the young male. The tiercel fed him.

I levelled my 'scope at the old falcon. By now she had scratched the creamy white plume off her head. She swooped down, copping on the tiercel's perch below the eyrie for the first time. Only the young male had a meal. The falcon returned to her perch in the rowan. She's done the prolonged graft of guarding and feeding

the brood. Very soon now, I thought, they'll be on the wing. I watched them clawing and heaving away from the scrape. They squatted yards apart on the buttress, their backs to the vale, difficult to identify as young peregrines. They are about 34 days old, virtually safe from thieves. The itch was in me to witness their maiden flights.

15th June: Into a downpour at 5.15 p.m. Located one of the eyases higher still on the rock face above the nest. The old birds hekked savagely, slashing about in rainy space close to the rim of the cirque. Afraid of causing a premature attempt from the youngsters, I slunk away back over the top. Tramping wet-legged to my crotch, I had a crude experience to warrant this retreat. It happened in Powys. A party of twenty climbers frightened the single eyas off the nest ledge. Luckily it crash-landed in heather. The fully accoutred climbers continued snailing up a ravine, either deaf to or jokily amazed at the frantic parent birds. I reported the incident to the N.C.C.—it was N.C.C. property. A topdog officer, Dr. something, sent me a genuine bullshit reply, saying there had been a breakdown in liaison between the climbing organisation and the Nature Conservancy Council. Shortly afterwards the N.C.C. stuck up a noticeboard, diverting the public from the crags with a long, long line of white marker posts. The assuaging niceness of bourgeois bureaucracies remains impenetrable.

16th June: Sunshine and cloud, the fearless falcon weaving above the cirque until I settled down. She perched in the dead rowan. At 5.20 p.m. the tiercel arrived from the far side. He disappeared over the top. Confidently enough, I searched for the eyases, tracking my 'scope in sawtooth sweeps across the basin. They weren't to be seen on the frontal ledges of the buttresses. The tiercel returned to a rowan tree in the larder gully. At 6.25 p.m. the falcon made a laborious kind of flight towards me. She perched on a nearside buttress, turned, and looked back at the nest ledge. Ten minutes later one of the eyases flew out from below the tiercel in the larder gully, winging a cool, sure semi-circle to the far end of Cerrig Fawr. The falcon went back to the dead rowan. The tiercel hadn't moved. It was half past six.

I searched for the other eyas. Rock, lichen, mosses, ivy, heather, whinberry, assorted montane plants exciting to the heads-down brigade of botanists, but no creature movement. I waited. Elemental tranquillity peculiar to high places. Gnats pinkened themselves on my neck and wrists. I waited, fearful. I felt like a self-designated Anglo-Welsh doppelganger of Franz Kafka: "Do not despair even if you do not despair." My hearing functioned sort of detached, clicking on shrilling swifts cutting unrepeatable mazes high overhead, on titlarks, skylarks, the graveyard *prukk-prukk* of a raven, magpie chatter, wren song reeling from the watershed, a coughing ewe somewhere behind me where the buttresses dribble out to the steep green gully with a twisted, rutted sheeptrack older than America. Again I peered through the 'scope. Nothing.

8.00 p.m. The missing eyas crept insectile over a ledge slightly above the perched tiercel. It was the young male. His whining has deepened, acquired a rasping timbre. He scrambled through the rowan foliage, rushing along the branch towards the tiercel. The tiercel slewed down to his old perch below the eyrie. The eyas bobbed his head. His long toes stretched and tightened on the bark. He roused, fluffing himself, his wings left hanging ajar. Another shake and he hunched into dopiness.

8.35 p.m., the great rough bowl of Cerrig Fawr cast in deep shade. Strolling back over the top, I flushed a titlark off five eggs. After stepping twenty paces due west, I searched the cloudless evening sky for crows or ravens, then I knotted grass stalks around a plastic sandwich bag. Corvids govern the bare hills. They are the supreme gimlet-eyed foragers, their survival triggered by minutiae. Inhabiting pitiless Arcadia, they cannot dream bygones or swoony beatitudes.

18th June: With Allan and Jim. Uncrusty old bachelor Jim, down from the Smoke for a week to watch peregrines, gourmetise and argue in pubs, quirky, niggling arguments once likened to *The Archers*, i.e. long-winded, '. . . except you and Jim blaspheme over aesthetics.' Our critic was an Eng.Lit. dilettante, a listener/participant who eventually floundered and lost interest, convinced we were incurable, meaningless, similar to *The Archers.* True I suppose; our mouthy analyses are cul de sac oriented.

Anyhow, rain drenched down shortly after we left the car, heavy stuff lashing across the face of Cerrig Fawr. We saw the tiercel standing a couple of yards above one of the eyases, not far from my watch-point below the rock shelf. Rain tamped, seething into every cranny on the buttresses. The tiercel screamed. We climbed down the steep green gully, down and around, skirting the scree at the base of the rocks. Jim tramped in the rear, unseeing, his head bent, cheerful though, as if native, a conqueror of wasteland, humming to himself, *"I'm an old cowhand from the Rio Grande."* The peregrines were quiet. Dampness seeped through our coats and leggings. I saw rain spatting off Allan's nose as he tried and failed to look up at the buttresses. Drips ran off his wiry beard. Tonguing his wet lips, he said, "We should have stayed in the car."

Jim slanted decorously on his (my) walking stick. "I'm relying on you blokes to get me back to civilisation."

We took a winding sheeptrack up the far side of the basin. A hillside has to pitch 1:2 for sheep to zigzag. They meander scrupulously around patches of upland quag. Straighter tracks lead to jumpable stream-crossings.

A spaced row of five low, grass-topped rock ledges are strung midway across the steep flank. We found some old and fresh pluckings on these ledges. Two pigeon-rings glimmered among the feathers, one a stout, rib-edged plastic ring which had been twisted and snapped off the pigeon's leg. Our fingers weren't so strong as the peregrine's notched bill. We could not break the plastic, stamped with the loft-owner's phone number and address, about fifteen crow-flight miles from Cerrig Fawr. Every grassy platform was decorated with pluckings, yet throughout my watching sessions only twice had I seen a peregrine pluming prey on these ledges. All pigeon kills, all the colours: checkers, blues, reds, mealies, grizzles. In the old days, during the Twenties, Thirties and Forties, the peregrines of Cerrig Fawr would have been downed by men with 12 bore shotguns, patient killers squatting in stone-built butts below the nest site; dusk coming on, the raptors blasted as they copped in. Shooting peregrines to protect racing-pigeons was endemic to South Wales as the traditional slaughter of peregrines on grouse moors, sanctioned by the same morality. From my own small locality, I knew half a dozen men who delivered riddled peregrines to pigeon-fanciers' clubs every season, for shillings. Most of them are now resting in the big butt in the sky. Times change, human nature holds true. Felons are now involved in deals with falconers and austringers, a kind of mafia conspiracy, gossip leaking out, sundering like froth, hints and innuendoes, names dropped from sources poisoned by envy, a quaky ethos of dedication, feuds, prideful ownership and cash. Elsewhere in the United Kingdom, ardent and often woefully innocent believers in the Nature Conservancy Council and the Royal Society for the Protection of Birds, not to mention before-and-after-dinner career chaps in the D. of E.

Straight rain hatched the atmosphere as we walked back to the car. Flinging his wet clothes into the boot, Jim went into a sotto voce rendering of "*Happy days, happy days, when Jesus washed my sins away.*"

Allan hung over the wheel. "Let's go, whacker," he said.

20th June: Intoxicating four-hour session with Allan. Both eyases on the wing inside the cirque. First we spotted a youngster lying flat on a flaked-off plate of rock above the eyrie. Farther away in the leafless rowan, the old falcon stood puffily lethargic. Presently, in fits and starts, the second eyas inched clear of the larder gully, launched out with precise grace, skimmed below us and banked away. The cream-tipped tail feathers were longer than those of a mature peregrine, fanning kestrelish as the eyas braked outside the bare rowan, the old falcon jogging her head as the youngster swooped down and up to a rock shelf—the genuine cop of a peregrine. Hawks (*Accipiter*) are long legged. Peregrines (*Falco*) have the rolling, stumpy-legged gait of a macaw. One time in '78, when I had a sandwich held to my mouth, a falcon pitched four yards from my boots. I stopped breathing, spittle drying behind my teeth (false) bedded in bread and bacon. She swivelled about-turn on the rock, the power of her evoking a twinge of dread, and as she heaved away I saw her short bandy legs below the close barring of her plus fours, the long butter-yellow, black taloned toes bunching, retracting. Memorable all right, a boggling fluke effected by/in time and space. It was late February, the birds were courting, prospecting Cerrig Fach for their nesting scrape.

Together and separately, the eyases made training-flights outside the buttresses. After about two hours the tiercel flew down from the larder gully. He went to his customary perch below the eyrie, screamed twice, abruptly dropped away, shaving the rocks, rose beyond the dead rowan and disappeared over the top. The old falcon drew up her right leg.

We were fascinated by the youngsters. Despite the slower feathering of the female eyas in the eyrie, both are on par as fliers. Being rather fanatical, I felt proud of them, ridiculous really because they weren't *mine.* To own a peregrine strikes me as ruinously banal, the prerogative only of nomads, reminders of the world before the written word, inevitably doomed to vanish off the face of the earth. Meanwhile we skedaddle towards 2,000 A.D. We have a far more expendable latter-day rash of feudal-minded, avaricious wheeler-dealers who spell peregrines as pelf. Captive born and reared raptors, under the scrutiny of shaman falconers, portends something else. Grotesques maybe, freaky falcon versions of tumbler pigeons, see-through gold-fish, battery chickens, Landrace pigs, pom-pom dahlias, bacteria, viruses. Altruism glitters in the eye of the controller. Neither are clocks turned back, for we are the stock of Australopithicus, Homo Erectus, Rhodesian man, Neanderthal man, Cro-Magnon and Upper Cave and Boscop man.

But still, we are beginning to learn that conservation does not mean 'management'. It means leaving be, stepping out of the skin of monomania, shedding nationhood and dogmas from on high, the huffs and puffs of consciousness buggered by realities. Of course murder and pillage have never been problems for Christians, for bare-footed multitudes kneeling to Allah, and breast-beating Kongs in charge of nuclear buttons, who see damn-all of the world in a grain of sand. Every nuclear scientist deserves a William Blake, as every psychoanalyst merits an accountant.

"Hey-hey-hey", muttered Allan as if talking to himself.

Crabbing sideways, the tiercel eyas dragged a partly plumed pigeon out onto a turfed ledge. We focused our 'scopes on him. A red checker pigeon, dabs of white on its breast and secondaries, the youngster tugging, switching these away with expertise, but less efficient when plucking bloodied underbelly and rump feathers. They stuck around his beak. He wobbled, changed his grasp one leg at a time. He funnelled his head in the soft feathers.

"Cached this morning," suggested Allan.

"He knew where to find it," I had to say.

"Imprinted," said Allan, "same as that young'un at Cerrig Fach, year before last."

While the youngster fed we recalled the incident. Allan's watch started at 6.30 a.m. I arrived an hour or so later. He saw the tiercel dropping a kill in a bed of rushes up in the right-hand corner of Cerrig Fach. The tiercel flew back across the rock face to his look-out perch. Allan did a fast, fit man's climb up to the rushes. It was a completely naked pigeon carcass, clean plucked as if ready for the oven, talon holes oozing thin smears of blood from the rosy flesh. Naturally he left it in the rushes. Right. Meanwhile, six days out of the nest, the Cerrig Fach eyas made a few flights between long rests and scampering about on the bushed ledges. The cloudless morning filled out to warm midday. The parent birds scarcely moved. Neatly sideways against blue pennant rock, they absorbed the sunshine. The tiercel came sailing out and around at 1.15 p.m., fluttered like a tern above the rushes, gathered up the carcass with one foot, then, immediately after he carried it across to the rock face, the head-bobbing eyas made a long, shallow swoop to ground-level, where a sheeptrack followed the edge of the scree, grabbed a dead cock blackbird from the short grass, proper fore and aft style, the blackbird's yellow beak glinting, and ferried it 400 yards to a wide rock shelf. The eyas rested, standing on the blackbird. One of the old birds had struck it down, or dropped it, before 6.30 a.m. when Allan arrived at Cerrig Fach.

The enigma remains. We still wonder how long memories stay imprinted on a peregrine's brain cells. Do they retain memories beyond/outside food and ancient eyrie sites? We have our yesterdays and our tomorrows. We celebrate, we grieve. A thought occurs: all the minuscule interlinked systems together making the existence of a peregrine are so organised as to make imagination unnecessary. We imagine for them, for cats and crocodiles, for dingoes and wombats, for elks and whales, drones and weevils, gnus and hedgehogs, our queerest burden metaphorically handed down from Eden.

Returning over the top, I stepped twenty paces from the grass-tied plastic bag to the titlark's nest. It was empty. Searching the equally empty sky, we picked up a tiny black freckle speeding under greying blue.

"The tiercel, sure to be," Allan said. "He's enjoying himself."

23rd June: Afternoon watch with Jim; both eyases superb on the wing. They practised stooping, compacting to bomb-shape, they flung up from each other within millimetres of contact. From our vantage point a yard below the skyline, we had comparatively (for these raptors) close-range viewing at eye level. Eleven

times in 90 minutes they talon-grappled, tumbling, their raucous screeching echoing Cerrig Fawr. Keeping her distance way out from the cirque, the falcon was a spectator for two hours. We saw the tiercel beyond the sparring youngsters, shooting down, down, vanishing below the far horizon.

The male eyas drilled himself, diving at the topmost, slender frond of a rowan. On his third strike he held tight, toppling head-down once, twice, three times, the leafy twig springing him upright. Then he let go, swerved out from the buttress, lofted as if bounced and threw down on a crow hunting for leather-jackets on the moorland. The crow squatted, beak raised. As the eyas keeled over for another stoop, the crow side-stepped adroitly as Phil Bennet. The eyas raked past, his right wing cuffing a budding spire of golden-rod. As always, a second crow appeared, batting along with intent over the moorland. The young peregrine had the sense to leave them alone.

The eyases rarely flew away from the cirque. We saw the young female fussing and pulling in the grass above the ivied buttress. Before leaving we walked around the curved brink of Cerrig Fawr. It was a clump of wool stained with the maggot-killing tarry paste which farmers daub under the tails of sheep.

2nd July: Two ravens crossing half a mile of open hillside, the eyases attacking, screech-bombing without snicking a black feather. The ravens simply plugged on, roll-flipping from their tormentors. Traditional education for the eyases. Ten seasons of watching peregrines at eyries, and I have yet to see them actually strike a raven. The billows-sounding *whooff-fooff whooff-fooff* of ravens' wings blew down after the eyases broke off, heading away into sultry haze, purposeful as mature peregrines. But they aren't independent of the parent birds. They have to learn to kill by the end of the summer.

The old falcon stood in the dead rowan. When the youngsters returned to the cirque, they harried her from all angles. She took them on for a while, chasing, flinging down, rising clear, winding up speed, stroking and gliding, leaving them in possession of Cerrig Fawr. As if bidden, the tiercel flew from the larder gully, a blue pigeon dangling from his left foot. He tempted and bullied his brood, but the youngsters failed to grasp the pigeon in mid-air. They spoiled each other. He released it, pitched into a vertical stoop and caught the flopping homer before it hit the ground. So he left it on a grassy (a smooth surface makes pluming more difficult) mound. The falcon eyas mantled over it, relaxed herself, clutching the pigeon, her open beak now and again creaking a long-drawn call. Twenty minutes went by before she began pluming the bird. The male eyas had disappeared in the larder gully.

A fleeting sprinkle of warm summer rain burnished the landscape, left it ethereal. Commando-writhing on elbows and knees, I sneaked my head over the craggy drop of the larder gully. The young tiercel was resting on his belly. Feathers garlanded every ledge. A necessary kind of carnage carnivalled the gully. Cerrig Fawr's Golgotha. Feathers disintegrate slower than grass.

7th July: The singular (for these parts) tootling of a lone curlew passing high over the tops. 7.25 p.m., the cirque lifeless, only insects moving, sucking Group A ichor from my neck, face and hands. Horseflies buzz softly inoffensive, they inject poison like dappled grey automata. The sun was a blank golden disc behind pallid gunmetal merging into bedsheet whiteness in the eastern sky. I found the shellbacked falcon, her beak to the blue pennant rock, her lower half concealed by a black frizz of dead heather.

Constant as fate, two crows probed among the parched tussocks down below. Distractions flaw peregrine-watching unless one's eyes and ears instantly connect back to the birds. The tiercel and the youngsters were hidden or absent. Four sheep were pale splodges lumping into legless silhouettes on the far, steep hillside. For no reason worth a farthing, I cannoned back half a century or more to my early adolescence. To nineteen dead ewes in a jumbled heap in one of the small house-coal levels pocking the mountainsides of South Wales. These levels were worked by penniless miners during the strikes of '21 and '26. Quixotic resurrection inside my head of a pre-War incident, some forgotten arctic Winter, the sheep seeking shelter, all perishing a few yards inside the old, collapsed level. My black and tan terrier refused to go in. I crawled in, striking matches. The stink, the awful pong of rotting mutton and spilt bowels. Later I held up a miner's carbide lamp while the farmer tallied his loss. Down in the farmhouse, his wife wept self-pity.

The Cerrig Fawr sheep straggled up and over the summit. I had already abandoned nit-picking for sequences to identify the particular Winter. Let it go. The farmer and his wife are also dead, and the chain of holes in the mountainside are buried under sitka spruces. Sitkas suit sparrowhawks, their secretive, snatching banditry. Peregrines are raptors of space, wide horizons. Roaming under all-weather skies, they are second best to myth, the undying phoenix. Studying peregrines in the wild, as I understand it, tends to unhinge one's cloistered humanity.

I tramped a longer route away from Cerrig Fawr. Dusk overfilled the vale, headlights fizzing on and off the roundabout like a space-age war-game for quick-witted children. I rested on my seat-stick, pivoting. From above the cirque half a mile away, the wrenching scream of a peregrine. Then silence, vacuity, a darkening maw engulfing subdued spurts of droning from the traffic.

9th July: Cerrig Fawr has changed, become prosaic and safe. The peregrines are gone. Two immature male kestrels sprayed out from the eyrie buttress, they phoophed skittishly like origami artifacts, they rode on zephyrs with impunity. They knew the peregrines' reign had ended. A family of magpies foraged along the lower ledges, looping squawking flights one after the other. I sat out in the open on top of the cirque. Twenty-two ravens were airborne together, many of them in moult, blackly tattered and labouring. They came down on the bare right-hand mountain above the alder wood, a sensible parliament of ravens. Cock titlarks and skylarks sang, their hens incubating second or third clutches. Wheatears fretted, chakking incessantly, feeding young scattered in patches of fern among the scree.

All over for this season, I thought. But where are they? The young peregrines aren't able to hunt efficiently. Without the parent birds they cannot survive.

Painfully cautious, I wriggled across a rock ledge to a quintet of well-used plucking stations. There were little owl feathers, lark, thrush, green woodpecker, jackdaw, blackbird, chaffinch, redpoll, wheatear, and seven delicate, lustrous green feathers off a budgie. Sifting among clogged pigeon feathers, I found four alloy rings. A couple of yards below, lodged in stalky heather, some buzzard primaries and tail feathers. The nearest breeding buzzards are eighteen miles from Cerrig Fawr.

I felt a sense of loss. Relief and loss.

21st July: Dog-day evening. I searched below the eyrie for pellets. They were hard to find among the lichened stones. No more pigeon rings. A mottled young ring-ouzel flew out from the larder gully. Spiralling high above the gully's canyon of sky, a buzzard mewed melancholy as a bedraggled kitten.

I climbed out of the cirque, sweat-soaked, vowing this would be my last visit until next March.

A few days later I located the young peregrines. They were a couple of miles away, roosting and hunting from the long escarpment overlooking the reservoir. The old birds were in attendance, as they say, until the first week of August, falcon or tiercel, never the pair together, and they were always perched when I saw them, while the flamboyant youngsters created mock battles around the buttresses.

Observing the break-up of a peregrine family is the toughest of all. On 31st August I found the adult peregrines occupying a pre-War site, a cirque twice the size of Cerrig Fawr and about five miles away—twelve by road. They were undemonstrative, becalmed in the aftermath of their season. I saw them making one spectacular, organised kill. Flying out from adjoining buttresses, tiercel high above the falcon, they simultaneously split asunder a flock of pigeons, isolating a fawn and white bird by sheer speed, the tiercel powering three stoops, the falcon pursuing from the rear, driving the victim closer to the rocks, and the falcon bound to the pigeon when it was barely a yard off the

ground. She plumed the bird on a sheep-cropped whinberry bed. The tiercel clipped across to his look-out stand halfway around the cirque.

Between 15th and 18th September the old birds left this pre-War site. The young birds stayed on the escarpment until early October. Shortly afterwards the parent birds took over the territory. They roosted and hunted from the escarpment all Winter. Following the pattern of recent years, they returned to Cerrig Fawr in the first couple of days of March 1983.

Full cycle . . . broken on 17th April '83, when thieves stole the clutch of eggs.